Handmade
# BREADS

# Handmade
# *BREADS*

Simple Techniques for Baking Better Bread

## Ciril Hitz

Photography by
Ron Manville

**APPLE**

First published in the UK in 2009 by
Apple Press
7 Greenland Street
London NW1 0ND
United Kingdom
www.apple-press.com

ISBN-13: 978-184543-303-1

10 9 8 7 6 5 4 3 2 1

Cover design: Janice Petrie
Interior design: Sandra Salamony
All photography: Ron Manville

Printed in Singapore

# Dedication

This book is dedicated to my children, Kira and Cailen.
Their unconditional love is more gratifying than the
best bread I have ever baked.

# Contents

# by Jeffrey Hamelman

THE WORLD DOESN'T SEEM TO BE SLOW-ING DOWN; at least, the human beings who inhabit it don't. More work, more stress, more demands on our time; many perhaps even feel disconnected from fundamental human links, as if something within us is cracked, almost broken. And so it seems ironic to see the great resurgence in bread baking in so many parts of the world. After all, with so much tugging at us, how can we find the time to bake for ourselves, for our family and friends?

We are emotive creatures, and we require fulfillment, both tactile and creative. When we enter the realm of bread, we find that the chatter of life slips away, that our hands regain their tender partnership with the breathing dough. We reunite with an ineffable and elemental connection that has been part of our shared heritage for thousands of years. When bread comes fragrant from our ovens, we are rewarded with a most marvelous experience of creation.

*Handmade Breads* is a friendly book, written by a friend of good bread. Ciril Hitz is an outstanding teacher, and he has distilled his years as an instructor into a book that is both good and earnest, one that will make it easy for readers to enter the kitchen with confidence. Ciril rolls up his sleeves from the first page and has us pulling out the flour. His approach will be especially helpful to those new to baking.

The recipes he offers are sound and solid, and the variations he gives for each of them enable us to really expand our repertoire. It's particularly valuable to be able to make good bread, a tasty savory item, and even a dessert from just one dough—a small increase in time and ingredients results in a large increase in products and flavors.

On their own, Ron Manville's photographs are absolutely delightful; when coupled with Ciril's discussions of themes such as shaping and troubleshooting, there is a synergy that vividly elucidates the topic. Habits, either good ones or bad, feel natural, and the combination of clear text and skilled photography will prove especially helpful to new bakers who are learning the basics, those whose habits have yet to be fully formed. Ciril has opened a door into a room full of many possibilities—your kitchen. His hope, which I fully share, is that you take the time to explore that room and expand your experience and your love of baking fine breads.

*Jeffrey Hamelman is an employee-owner of the King Arthur Flour Company in Norwich, Vermont. He is the director of the King Arthur Bakery, and instructs the professional classes offered at the King Arthur Baking Education Center. He is the author of* Bread: A Baker's Book of Techniques and Recipes.

# The Quest for Handmade Bread

FLOUR, WATER, SALT, AND YEAST—these four simple ingredients when combined create the magic that is bread. Baking bread is a time-honoured tradition honed over more than six thousand years. The craft is a truly sensory experience: the warmth of the dough in your hands, the aromas lingering in the air during baking, the crackling of the crust as it cools, the complex and seductive flavours on your tongue. Yet for some, the process of making bread strikes fear in their hearts. I hope to change that.

The good news is that the quest to make good bread by hand is not one of endless toil. Technology is the baker's friend, and mixers and other equipment are welcome time-savers. It is my opinion that a baker can craft "handmade" bread while taking advantage of helpful technology. Time is also a critical ingredient that cannot be shortchanged.

Being organized and rational about the baking process will aid the aspiring baker. When I competed in my first international baking competition, I streamlined my baking style to maximize my performance and products within a limited amount of time. As a result, I've learned to work through geometric expansion, increasing the number of different breads that can be made from one dough.

My premise is simple: If you are going to invest the ingredients, time, and energy in making a dough from scratch, then why not maximize this effort to

*With these formulas, you can create a multitude of*

create more bread? After all, isn't time one of our most precious resources? With just small adjustments or additions, each of the ten bread formulas in *Handmade Breads* generates a new bread form. A baguette dough yields a bouquet of breadsticks, a buttery brioche dough elegantly becomes a fruit danish, and so on, through more than thirty mouth-watering variations.

*Handmade Breads* provides clear definitions, thorough explanations, and logical steps for creating wonderful bread at home with professional-quality results. The main ingredients are introduced and pored over in chapter 1, while chapter 2 introduces the basic necessary equipment, along with some essential techniques and concepts. These two chapters of part 1 pave the way for part 2, beginning with chapter 3, an overview of the ten steps of baking that provides the organisational thrust of each formula. This chapter introduces what happens at each stage of the dough development and why—what mixing really is, why a dough needs to rest, and when it is ready to bake. It is followed by the formulas and variations, presented in lush, step-by-step photos. If by then you haven't become a disciple of bread baking, it is my hope that with time and practice, you will revel in its joys as much as I do.

Happy baking!

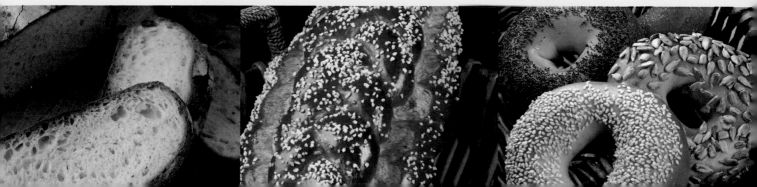

fantastic, flavourful breads for any occasion.

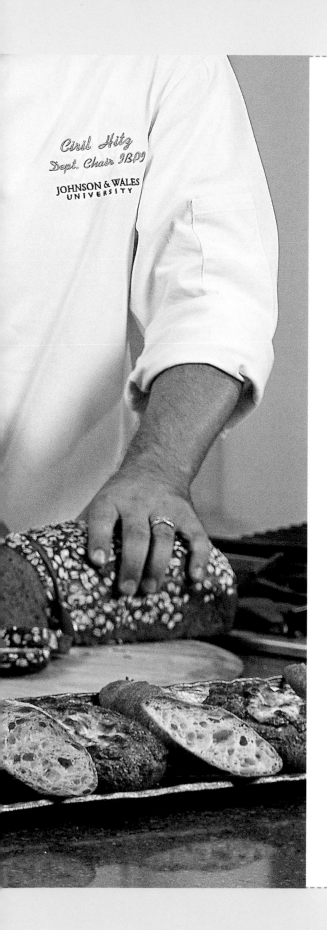

# PART ONE

# Basics

BREAD BAKING is a delicate dance between the simple and the complex. On one hand, nothing could be more straightforward: just combining flour, water, salt, and yeast yields a dough that with the baker's touch magically transforms into a crusty baguette or a hearty loaf. On the other hand, the science behind the "magic" is incredibly complicated, and research reveals the markedly complicated process that baking actually is.

Don't let the complexities of the baking process intimidate you, though. Knowledge is power and, in the case of bread baking, an overview of the components and processes is all you need to start your journey. In the following chapters, the roles of the ingredients, equipment, and techniques are explained and expounded upon. The most important information is extracted and reduced to readily accessible and easily understood core concepts. Armed with these essentials, you can move confidently into the kitchen and let the baking begin!

# CHAPTER ONE

# Ingredients

**THE MAIN INGREDIENTS** of bread are strikingly simple: flour, water, salt, and yeast. Each one has a precise role to play in creating a dough that has the qualities desired in the type of bread.

Using the highest quality ingredients you can afford is one of the keys to successful baking. Creating the best product possible starts with the best possible ingredients. These are, after all, the foundation of any formula, and sacrifices or compromises made at this level will definitely have an impact on the bread. That being said, you should not take out a second mortgage to get through your shopping list. One of the great things about bread baking is that the basics are very common and usually do not involve extra trips to specialty foods stores.

For some, though, shopping is half the fun. If you are someone who pores over kitchen product catalogs, or you incessantly comb the Internet for new and interesting sources of little-known ingredients, then by all means, experiment! Experimenting with different brands of flour or yeast will be part of your education as a baker. As you gain experience, you will develop your own baking identity and personal preferences and will come to recognise the qualities of ingredients (and their edible results) that are most important. Baking bread is an art form, one that is open to interpretation and individualizing. And so while each formula has certain standards to be met, bakers bring their own set of unique tools and ideas, ready to make their individual mark on their bread.

The next few pages introduce and explore the four basic ingredients used to make bread. While the main points of each ingredient are simplified, some are more complex than others. Flour, for example, has many different characteristics that a baker must take into consideration when choosing one. Water, on the other hand, does not. As you read about each ingredient, you will become more aware of the choices available to you and what kind of issues may affect your purchases and baking decisions.

# Flour

Most bread consumed in the United States is made from wheat flour. Wheat is considered a cereal grain, along with rice, corn, oats, and rye. What makes wheat the grain of choice for bread baking? One of the primary factors is the presence of certain proteins with *gluten*-forming properties. When mixed with water and developed into dough, the wheat flour is given life, and the gluten protein creates a structure much like an intricate web. The interlaced gluten strands capture the gases that have been created by the yeast and are flexible enough to allow the dough to "rise," expanding in size.

## HOW FLOUR IS MADE

Flour is made by grinding wheat kernels, also known as wheat berries. A wheat kernel is the seed of the wheat plant and has three main parts: the *bran*, the *endosperm*, and the *germ*. The bran is the outer protective layer of the kernel and is high in insoluble fiber, minerals, and vitamin B. Underneath the bran lies the endosperm, which makes up the bulk of the kernel. It contains mostly starch and is the whitest part of the kernel. It also contains the proteins that form the gluten matrix, a necessary component of a bread's crumb structure. Most refined flour comes from this part of the kernel. The germ, in the right conditions, will sprout, or germinate, and allow

A variety of flours and wheat, clockwise: pastry flour, bread flour, high-gluten flour, white whole wheat flour, cracked wheat; middle: whole wheat berries

the seed to grow into a new plant. This embryo is composed of essential oils and vitamin E.

Wheat is made into flour by milling. The wheat kernel is crushed into progressively smaller particles, and depending on the type of flour, parts of the kernel are removed by sifting. The degree of separation that takes place is called the *extraction rate*. A flour that uses the entire wheat kernel is said to have a 100 percent extraction rate, meaning the entire kernel was ground into flour and nothing was removed, resulting in a 100 percent whole wheat flour. Most conventional bread flours have an extraction rate of 73 to 76 percent. As a rule, flour with a higher extraction rate contains more minerals and is more nutritious than flour with a lower rate.

By law, supplements can be added to the flour to replace any vitamins and minerals removed during the milling process. This, however, does not replace the nutritional benefit of whole-grain flour.

Once flour is milled, it needs time to mature. This aging process is critical to the performance of the flour in the baking cycle. Although unaged flour has more available nutrients, without proper aging flour tends to have a sluggish fermentation cycle and becomes harder to shape. Ideally, flour will have a minimum of 3 to 4 weeks to mature, which means storing the flour in large silos and taking up precious space. To mitigate the high costs of properly maturing flour, some suppliers artificially age the flour with gases and oxidizing agents such as potassium bromate. These agents have harmful side effects on both humans and the environment. The nutritional label on the flour is a good source of information about the manufacturers' aging processes. (It is advisable to choose unbleached and unbromated flour.)

## FLOUR SPECIFICATIONS

When bakers get together, they like to talk about their flour in very technical terms. For the home

## More Minerals = BETTER FERMENTATION

Just like the human body, yeast is a living organism that thrives when it is fed a good, healthy diet. The more minerals retained in the flour after milling, the more beneficial it is to the fermentation process. The nutrients present are processed by the yeast and result in a healthier, more robust culture.

baker, it is good to be aware that these specifications exist, but it is not necessary to be bogged down with or intimidated by this data, either. There are many different types of wheat: from hard to soft, from summer to winter, and from red to white. Each type of wheat has its own characteristics, and different flours are often blended to meet a certain specification. The bread flour preferred for the recipes in this book should be derived from a hard winter wheat. This type of wheat has a protein content between 11 and 14 percent, with the most ideal protein content for artisan bread baking being 11.5 to 11.7 percent. When held in the hand and squeezed, this flour does not lump up and does not need to be sifted.

## STORING FLOUR

Flour should be stored in an airtight container and away from heat. It is best to buy flour in quantities that will last around 2 to 3 months. Flour can also be wrapped tightly in plastic wrap and stored in the freezer for up to 1 year. Special consideration should be taken when storing whole wheat flour. The natural oils in the wheat germ make this flour more sensitive to heat than regular bread flour or all-purpose flour is. It is best to store this flour in an airtight container in the refrigerator, especially during warm spells, to prevent the flour from becoming rancid.

# Yeast

Yeast is a single-cell organism that feeds from simple sugars naturally present in flour in a process called *fermentation*. In the presence of warmth (ideally 75°F to 78°F [24°C to 26°C]) and moisture, this process takes place and accelerates with higher temperatures. The bread baker strives to enhance the flavour and aroma of the bread by controlling this process of fermentation.

## VARIETIES OF BAKING YEAST

There are innumerable types of yeast, but two are specifically used for fermenting bread: the wild *Candida milleri* and the manufactured *Saccharomyces cerevsiae*. Sourdough breads are made with the wild yeast, and the baker maintains the yeast's life cycle by regularly feeding the sourdough culture, also known as a starter. The care and cultivation of starters and their use in baking is more complicated and challenging than the scope of this book, and therefore none of the formulas presented in this book are for sourdough breads. Instead, these formulas utilize manufactured yeast that is produced in a lab facility under very tight and strict conditions.

Commercial yeast is available in three main forms:

### Active Dry Yeast

Until recently, active dry yeast was practically the only yeast one could buy in a supermarket. Usually sold in packaged perforated envelopes, active dry yeast needs to be rehydrated properly before use. The yeast is allowed to dissolve for about 5 minutes in 100°F (38°C) liquid (water in most cases) before being added to the final dough. If the formula calls for water to be at a cooler temperature when it is added to the final dough, the liquid yeast solution should be cooled before the mixing can commence.

From top to bottom: active dry, instant, and fresh yeast

## FERMENTATION 101

The complicated process of fermentation, reduced to bare bones, goes something like this: The starches present in flour are broken down into simple sugars, which then act as food for the yeast. The yeast "eats" the sugar and expels carbon dioxide and alcohol in the process. This feeding cycle continues until the yeast runs out of sugar, or until the bread is baked. Once the internal temperature of 138°F (59°C) is reached, known to bakers as the "thermal death point," all fermentation ceases. One can almost picture the tiny molecules of carbon dioxide gas trying to make their way out of the dough, but the gluten matrix (that weblike structure of gluten forming proteins) traps the gas, creating a balloon around the carbon dioxide. This gives the dough the desired rising characteristic typical for yeasted breads. (The gluten-forming process is explored at length in chapter 2, pages 29–30.) The alcohol dissipates during the baking process.

### Instant Yeast

Sometimes marketed by manufacturers as "bread machine yeast," instant yeast is usually sold in a small vacuum-packed brick and is available in many larger supermarkets and through catalog and Internet sources. It has a long shelf life and can be stored unopened without refrigeration for up to a year. Once opened, it should be stored in an airtight container in the refrigerator. Although the manufacturers recommend that it be used within a month, it can usually be stored *much* longer. The beauty of instant yeast is that it can be added directly to the dry ingredients of the final dough before mixing. While it may be a bit pricier than fresh yeast, the dependability of its performance far outweighs the additional cost.

Instant yeast is also available in an *osmotolerant* form for use in sweeter, enriched doughs. The abundant sugar present in these doughs draws the water away from the yeast, making it a very inhospitable environment for regular instant yeast to do its job. The osmotolerant form has literally been engineered to perform under these harsh conditions and is therefore ideal to use in sweet and enriched yeasted doughs, such as brioche (see page 124).

### Fresh Baker's Yeast

Fresh, or compressed, yeast contains 70 percent water. It is tan in colour and should break cleanly when touched. It should have a pleasant, yeasty odor to it. Fresh yeast can be purchased at some grocery stores and through catalog and Internet sources and should be stored in an airtight container in the refrigerator, where it has a shelf life of 3 weeks. A drawback of fresh yeast for home bakers is that one can never be quite certain if the yeast is actually fresh enough, especially if it is purchased from a source that does not sell much on a regular basis. Even most experienced, professional bakers tend to prefer the more consistent quality and performance of instant yeast.

The formulas in this book specify instant yeast exclusively, as it is a favourite ingredient both at home and in the bakeshop. If you would like to experiment with either active dry or fresh yeast, please refer to the yeast conversion chart in the appendix (page 165).

# Water

When it first comes in contact with flour, water swells the starches and awakens the dormant gluten-forming proteins. Fermentation could not take place without water and, to ferment properly, the dough needs to achieve a certain temperature. The temperature of the flour and any pre-ferments are dictated by their surroundings and are hard to change. The temperature of the water is the only variable that can easily be adjusted before it is added to the final dough to help ensure that it reaches the necessary temperature range.

## HYDRATION RATES of Dough

Water is the main hydrating factor in dough, although other liquids are frequently included, such as milk, eggs, and oils. When bakers talk about the *hydration* of doughs, they are referring to the relationship between the liquids as they compare to the flour. For example, if a dough has 1,000 grams of flour and 750 grams of liquid, it has a hydration rate of 75 percent. A dough with a high hydration will be wet and sticky, whereas a dough with a low hydration will be stiffer. If a dough has too much liquid (more than 80 percent hydration), it will be too wet to comfortably handle. On the flip side, a dough must have a minimum hydration of 50 percent or the dough will not come together as a unified mass.

Tap water is the preferred water to use, but certain variables should be kept in mind because of their impact on the dough. For example, water containing too much chlorine will tend to slow down the fermentation process. If water smells like chlorine, it is best to pre-scale it and let it sit at room temperature until the odor dissipates. Minerals present in the water will not usually interfere with baking. If the water is too hard, the overabundant minerals can actually accelerate the fermentation process (although this is most evident when working with sourdough cultures and not with commercial yeast). Working with distilled water is not recommended, since it has been stripped of minerals. (And in case you are wondering, you can certainly make bread with bottled spring water—but it simply does not make good financial or environmental sense.)

# Salt

Even though it is used in such minute amounts, salt is an essential ingredient with a critical role in bread baking. Most might assume that salt is added for its flavour, which is not entirely false: Salt does add to the flavour of bread. It should never dictate the flavour, however; instead it should complement the flavour of a well-fermented loaf.

Salt's primary function is something completely distinct from flavour: It helps control the fermentation process, preventing the yeast from overfermenting. An uncomplicated way to say it is the enzymatic reaction of salt in the dough actually encourages the slower digestion of the sugars. In return, not all of the sugars are consumed by the yeast, and the ones that are still present at the time of baking become evident as they caramelize into the golden-brown colour on the crust. Salt also has an effect on the proteins by tightening them up, which is evident in the final dough.

## TYPES OF SALT

Salt comes in many forms, including sea salt, kosher salt, and regular table salt. Any type can be used in bread baking, as long as the granule size is fine enough to disperse and dissolve properly in the dough. When adding ingredients and especially if you are pre-scaling ingredients to hold overnight, always make sure that the salt and the yeast do not come in contact with each other; salt's potency has the potential to damage

A variety of salts from left to right: coarse sea salt, fine sea salt, table salt, and kosher salt

# CHAPTER TWO

# Equipment and Techniques

BREAD IS MADE with the simplest of tools, including the hands and a source of fire. As bread baking evolved, so did how it was made. Through modern technology, machines and tools eased the arduous work of the baker. There was great resistance to newfangled machinery in Europe, particularly in France, where bakers were steeped in the traditional art of hand kneading.

Over time, bakers relented and by the 1920s electric ovens, fast-rising yeasts, and mechanical mixers became the norm. Unfortunately, this "modern" approach did nothing to improve bread's quality, and it slipped into a manufactured state: soft, white, and tasteless. Fortunately, the handmade bread movement is encouraging more judicious choices of tools and equipment.

The most critical piece of equipment for any baker—and it may not seem like equipment—is the hands. Their dense concentrations of nerve endings register the minutest of tactile changes. No machine or tool will ever replicate this. Moreover, this "finger feel" only improves with time and experience! Every time you bake, the brain catalogues these sensations into an innate baking reference.

This chapter reviews the basic equipment you will need to bake handmade bread. If you are well equipped, you already have most of these items in your kitchen. If not, the next most important piece of equipment is a scale, followed by a stand mixer, followed by a baking stone. The qualities to look for in each of these pieces, along with others, are highlighted.

If you are a beginner or have limited experience in baking, the sections outlining pre-ferment basics and basic shaping techniques (see pages 42–47) will be most helpful in your tutorial. These sections are important reference points as you move through the formulas in the book.

## Basic MISE EN PLACE Equipment for All Formulas

Work surface
Stand mixer with a dough hook attachment
Mixing bowl
Proofing containers
Scale or measuring cups/spoons
Scraper/dough divider
Parchment paper
Thermometer
Oven
Wire cooling racks

## Scales and Measuring

While many aspects of bread baking are creative and artistic, baking is first and foremost a science. Accurately measuring the ingredients is a critical part of bread baking. Just as you would not conduct a scientific experiment using pinches of chemicals, nor should you approach measuring your ingredients in the same manner. Home bakers in the United States are understandably conditioned to measure their ingredients in spoons and cups. Unfortunately, this is a proven inferior way to measure consistently. The arguments against this method are many, ranging from the discrepancies in the manufacturing of the tools, to the different densities to which each individual fills the cups, to the dirty utensils to clean afterward. Weighing ingredients is simply much more accurate and uncluttered—case closed.

Measuring by weight is more accurate than measuring by volume.

## TYPES OF SCALES

Second to hands, a scale is the most important piece of equipment for a baker to have. Three different types of scales are available to the home baker:

### Balance Scales

The balance scale works by comparing the ingredient to be weighed against a known mass. The ingredient to be weighed is placed on one side of the scale, and weights are either placed on the opposite side or moved along a beam until the two sides are in balance. You have probably used a balance scale if you have ever taken a chemistry class, or when you have stepped on a physician's scale at the doctor's office. These scales can be extremely accurate but occupy a lot of space and are a bit cumbersome to use in the kitchen.

### Mechanical/Compression Scales

These scales use a platform mounted on a spring to measure weight: As the platform is compressed from the weight of the ingredient, the spring compresses proportionally to the force being applied to it. In theory this way of measuring works fine, but in reality there are some problems with mechanical scales, especially cheaply made ones. For example, compression rates may change over time, as the spring may stop fully returning to its original length, or it may even break. Another issue is that smaller quantities are more difficult for the scale to weigh accurately than larger quantities. (Have you ever wondered why that single onion at the supermarket weighs almost as much as two?)

### Digital Scales

Digital scales, the preferred equipment for these formulas, are easy to use and very accurate in the kitchen. Inside the scale is a small computer that calculates the weight based on the resistance measured on the strain gauge, a small electrical component. These scales are readily available at department and kitchen stores, as well as catalog and Internet sources, and range in price from affordable to slightly pricey. In general, the precision of the scale directly correlates to its price. For home bread baking, a scale with a 5-kilogram capacity (5,000 grams) that can weigh increments of 1 gram is recommended.

## WEIGHT CONVERSION FORMULA

To convert grams into ounces, divide the number of grams by 28.35.

**Example:** 72 grams = 2.54 ounces
72 ÷ 28.35 = 2.539

To convert ounces into grams, multiply the number of ounces by 28.35.

**Example:** 6 ounces = 170.1 grams
6 x 28.35 = 170.1

If an ingredient's measurement includes both pounds and ounces, first convert the pounds to ounces (multiply the number of pounds by 16), add the remaining ounces to that figure, and then multiply the answer by 28.35.

**Example:** 2 pounds 3 ounces = 992.25 grams
[(2 x 16) + 3] x 28.35 = 992.25

Here are some other scale features to consider:

- **Imperial and metric units:** All formulas and measurement for the ingredients in this book use the metric system; not all cookbooks or recipes do. It is nice to have a scale that can switch from kilograms and grams to pounds and ounces.

- **Tare function:** The tare function weighs the container and then zeros the scale so that only the net weight of the next added ingredient is displayed. Many scales allow repeated tares, which makes weighing multiple ingredients consecutively in the same bowl a snap. For

example, you can scale 500 grams of flour, press the tare button, scale 15 grams of salt, press the tare button again, and add 7 grams of yeast—all into the same bowl, without a single measuring utensil.

## SPOONS AND CUPS

The only truly accurate way to measure ingredients is by weight, not by volume (measuring with spoons and cups). If a scale is not available, use the following tips as a guide.

- **Flour:** There is no need to sift bread flour before measuring. Scoop the flour from its bin with the measuring cup, then level off the flour with the back of a knife.

- **Water:** Use a measuring cup made for measuring liquids (transparent glass or plastic cups with measured increments on the side, with a handle and a spout). Place the cup on a flat, level surface and read the measurement of the liquid at eye level.

- **Salt and instant yeast:** Use good-quality measuring spoons and level with the back of a knife.

Even when these measuring tips are followed with the utmost consistency, the characteristics of certain ingredients make this method unreliable. The density of flour can change from bag to bag, not to mention the fact that everybody scoops flour a little differently. Finely ground table salt will pack in tighter than coarsely ground sea salt, and so a tablespoon of fine table salt will weigh more (and flavour more!) than a tablespoon of coarse sea salt.

Tools used for measuring by volume should be of the highest quality to ensure accuracy.

# Philosophy of Baking:
## MEASURING INGREDIENTS

*To weigh or not to weigh?* That is the question. Or should it be? After being immersed in the industry for so long, it's hard for me to imagine measuring ingredients any other way. Quite simply, doling out ingredients by weight, and not by volume, is the most accurate measuring method. Many home bakers and cooks in Europe use a scale in the kitchen, particularly when measuring dry ingredients that can pack and settle. Most cookbooks on their shelves don't call for volume measurements. It is time for everyone else to start a grassroots baking revolution—put down those cups and spoons and get a scale!

Not only is weighing more accurate, but it is faster, too. Once the bowl has been tared on the scale, the first ingredient is added to the bowl until its weight is reached. Zero or tare the scale, then add the next ingredient, and repeat. Imagine: a world of baking free of honey-coated spoons, rubber scrapers, and measuring cups.

If you do consider the switch, you may as well consider adopting metrics while you are at it. No more fractions. No more trying to remember how many cups are in a pint (or are in a quart). All metric units are based on multiples of ten. The gram is a tiny measurement, and even that can be divided into milligrams for extreme precision. When you've purchased your baking scale and are ready to dive into these formulas, give the metric measurements a try and see for yourself.

Baking is an art as well as a science. While we are not trying to land a rocket on the moon, resorting to "pinches" and "dashes" just doesn't do justice to the science of baking. Celebrity chefs may be dramatically liberal with ingredients, but any culinary instructor will admit that there is more wiggle room in the kitchen than there is in the bakeshop.

# Mixers and Mixing

The process of mixing ingredients can take many different forms. Although each may take a different route, they all end up at the common destination: a properly-developed dough.

### HAND MIXING

Bread has been mixed by hand for thousands of years, and aspects of modern European culture were centred on the skill of the baker's touch. There is something very satisfying and meditative about the process, and many people deliberately choose to hand mix for this experience, despite its being so labor intensive. (In my own baking I use a mixer, but even then I constantly have my fingers in the dough—when the mixer is off, of course!) Nothing can replace the direct contact of skin to dough and the information that is transferred through the sense of touch. It is tiresome, though, mixing and kneading all that dough, especially if you are making more than just a couple of loaves. And certain doughs enriched with butter, such as brioche (see page 124), are very difficult to mix by hand, requiring a professional level of expertise.

One approach to hand mixing is to first incorporate the ingredients in a mixing bowl, using a bowl scraper or dough whisk. As the dough starts to come together, remove the dough from the bowl and work it on the table. Press down on the dough with both hands and push out away from you. Roll it back on top of itself and rotate it a quarter turn before starting the process again.

Other bakers use a slap and roll technique in which the dough is slapped down onto the table and then rolled back, picked up and slapped again (and again, and again…). Try both methods and see which one works better for you—you may decide to use the slap and roll technique for wetter doughs and the other for regular, stiffer doughs. The choice is completely a personal one.

Hand mixing (left) and kneading (bottom, left). The final dough (below) is stretched a bit to show its smooth, well-developed structure.

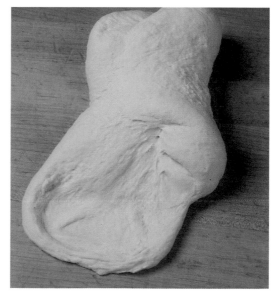

## FOOD PROCESSOR

Many home bread bakers use the food processor when mixing their doughs, and it can yield great results. The key is to mix in short bursts using the pulse mode instead of long cycles. Making bread with a food processor is a specialized technique, and several books have been devoted to it (see the Recommended Reading section, page 169).

## ELECTRIC STAND MIXER

The classic stand mixer, also called a planetary mixer, has a hook attachment that spins on an axis and rotates around a stationary bowl (much like a planet orbits the sun—thus the name). While this action can abuse the dough, it has its advantages. First, it saves the baker the energy of mixing by hand, and second, it allows the baker extra time to attend to other tasks while the dough is in the mixer.

All of the formulas in this book were developed with a stand mixer. With models ranging widely in price, it can be an expensive addition to the kitchen, but it is definitely worth the "dough" if you plan to do a lot of bread baking. New equipment is constantly being developed,

so it is best to inform yourself before making such a substantial purchase.

A 5-quart (5 L) bowl is the minimum size you should get; some mixers have 6- and 7-quart (6 and 7 L) models. The dough hook should have a complex bend to it, not just a graceful curve. This shape creates a more efficient mixing motion and will bring a dough together in less time. If the dough hook is poorly designed, mixing will take longer and the temperature of the dough will rise from the increased friction.

## ELECTRIC SPIRAL MIXER

This type of mixer is mostly available in larger professional capacities, although smaller versions of spiral mixers (8-pound [4 kg] dough capacity) have recently been introduced (at quite a hefty price tag!). The action of the spiral mixer mimics the hand kneading motion with its rotating dough hook and simultaneously turning bowl. It merits mentioning, since this is by far the gentlest way to develop a gluten matrix and is the most efficient way to mix a bread dough, with the dough developing in about half the time as on a stand mixer.

### The Incredible WALKING MIXER

Always keep an eye on your mixer! Depending on the mixer's capacity and strength and the type of dough being mixed, the force exerted during mixing can cause the mixer to shake, rattle, and roll. Some even develop the ability to "walk" across the counter and could end up on the floor if left unattended, obviously something you want to avoid. Putting a damp hand towel under the base of the mixer can help stabilize the mixer.

### NEVER JUDGE A MIXER by Its Wattage

Beware of judging a mixer by its wattage. Companies market their mixers as extra powerful, touting wattages as high as 1,000. This is simply a marketing gimmick. This number refers to the input wattage, the watts flowing into the mixer from the power source, not the output wattage, or the amount of power the motor actually produces. Essentially these numbers are irrelevant, as there is no correlation between wattage and the mixer's performance.

# Three Mixing Styles

Mixing brings together the flour, water, salt, and yeast (and any other ingredients) to form a homogenous mass. There are three distinct styles of mixing, all of which include an initial stage called the *cleanup stage,* which lasts 3 to 4 minutes in a stand mixer. The ingredients are brought together in a uniform consistency with very little gluten development. As the dough is mixing in this stage, the baker observes its development carefully—this is the stage where adjustments can be made to the dough relatively easily. Many professional bakers will not add all of their liquid, holding back 2 to 4 percent until they can determine that the flour is able to absorb it all. It is common for flour stored in a dry kitchen to absorb greater quantities of water than flour stored under humid conditions. After the dough has been adjusted as necessary and it has reached the cleanup stage, one of the following mixing styles is chosen, depending on the type of dough being mixed.

## SHORT MIX

The short mix mimics the hand-mixing technique used before the industrialization of mixing, when the majority of doughs were developed without machines. After the cleanup stage, the dough is mixed for an additional 1 to 2 minutes on a medium or second speed setting. When a dough is mixed with the short-mix method, it should have a

## GLUTEN WINDOW Test

Performing a simple gluten window test will indicate how much the gluten has developed during mixing. Take a piece of dough in your hands and slowly stretch it out. The more the gluten has developed, the farther the "web" will stretch before breaking. The window will vary depending on the type of dough and mixing. Here you see the three different types of mixing and the respective windows developed:

Short mix with little gluten development

Improved mix with almost full gluten development

Intensive mix with a full gluten development

very long bulk fermentation that allows for plenty of stretch and folds to ensure the proper gluten formation. This technique gives the creamiest of crumb and the most flavour potential from the flour, but it also requires the greatest number of hand manipulations through stretch and folds.

### IMPROVED MIX

Many bakeries use this method in their production. After reaching the cleanup stage, the dough is mixed for an additional 2 to 4 minutes on a medium or second speed setting. With an improved mix, a stronger gluten is developed with the dough on the mixer (yet not overdeveloped), and an almost perfect window test (see Gluten Window Test, page 31) can be performed. The dough should be completely smooth and have a slight shine to it.

### INTENSIVE MIX

An intensive mix is a much longer mix and is usually only used when mixing enriched doughs, or doughs that contain sugar and fats. Both sugar and fat have a tenderizing effect on the gluten structure. For this reason, the dough is mixed for a longer time to allow the overdevelopment of gluten, which compensates for this tenderizing factor. After the initial cleanup stage, the dough is mixed for an additional 4 to 15 minutes, depending on the efficiency of the mixer. The dough should come together with a good window test before any fats, usually butter, are incorporated. Once a good window has been formed and the butter has been made pliable through hammering with a rolling pin, the butter can slowly be added to the dough in stages. In the end, a thin and perfect window test can be performed.

## STRETCH-AND-FOLD
## Sequence

Some doughs require a series of stretches and folds to develop their strength. To perform a proper stretch and fold, place the dough on the table in front of you. Take the right end of the dough, gently stretch it out, and then fold it back one-third over itself. Do the same thing with the left side. Now take the edge closest to you and repeat the process, pulling the dough gently toward you and then folding it away from you and back onto itself. Continue this motion a little further, lifting up the corners of the fold and bringing the folded edge to meet the back edge. Pick up the dough and gently place, seam side down, into the proofing container.

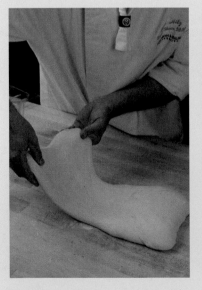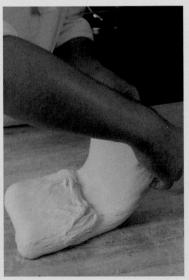

Manipulating the dough with a stretch-and-fold sequence

**A few general notes on mixing:**

• As noted on page 30, always pay attention to your mixer. If you are mixing a dough, it is not the time to hang the laundry or run a letter out to the mailbox. If something comes up that requires your attention, turn off the mixer.

• Any additional ingredients, such as seeds, nuts, berries, or fruits, should be added to the dough at the very end of the mixing stage. Adding them at the beginning of the cycle will disturb the gluten from developing properly.

• Whenever you are finished mixing a dough, take its temperature using a temperature probe.

The temperature of the dough as it comes off the mixer will be an indicator of how the fermentation will progress. If the dough is in the ideal range of 75°F to 78°F (24°C to 26°C), then you can proceed as the formula tells you. A lower temperature will slow down fermentation, and a higher temperature will speed up the process. A seasoned baker will know to make some adjustments, such as lengthening the bulk fermentation time or placing the dough in a warmer or cooler environment for a period of time.

*Note: Mixing times may vary, depending on the mixer, the ingredients, and the surrounding environment.*

# Other Tools

A number of other tools are helpful when baking handmade bread:

### BAKING MOLDS AND PANS

It is great when you have the exact size called for in a formula, but that is not always the case. Always try to work with what you have, but buy new pans if you feel it is necessary. Generally, the finished yeasted product will be approximately just more than twice the size of the dough before the final proof. Nonstick molds and pans are better for their ease of release and cleaning, but any quality molds or pans will work.

### BENCH SCRAPER

A plastic bench scraper with a long straight edge (not to be confused with a curved bowl scraper, see page 35) works wonders on the work space.

Top to bottom: Brioche forms, lidded Pullman pan, round baking form, and rectangular loaf pan

A metal bench scraper and a curved, plastic bowl scraper

## COUCHE

Couches are tightly woven textiles traditionally made of linen, a fabric composed of long and tightly spun fibers that easily release from the dough. They are used both to cover the dough during different parts of the proofing cycles and to aid in the separation and support of preshaped dough forms. Fancy French couches can be purchased at specialty stores and sources, or you can make your own. Sizes can vary, but an average couche measures 18 x 30 inches (46 x 75 cm).

### Making a Couche

Purchase a suitable length of fabric at an art supply store; it is is sold as either linen canvas or Egyptian linen. Hem the raw edges so loose fibers do not get stuck on the dough.

Never, *ever* wash the couches. To clean off excess flour and dough particles, scrape the surfaces with the edge of a plastic bench scraper and hang dry to remove any residual moisture from the dough. Tightly woven cotton kitchen towels also work, especially once the flour is worked into the fibers.

The straight edge on the bench scraper is slightly sharpened, making it effective for dividing dough and scraping dough off the table. Metal bench scrapers work just as well, but care must be taken not to damage their edge, or it might just damage your work surface.

## BOWL SCRAPER

A bowl scraper is a handheld, flexible contoured piece of plastic used to scrape ingredients off the insides of the mixing bowl. A rubber spatula can also be used for this purpose.

## COOLING RACK

A wire cooling rack is essential; it is the only way to surround a baked product with airflow to ensure proper cooling.

A couche dusted with flour

Baking stones are designed to mimic a hearth surface.

### HEARTH OR BAKING STONE

A hearth stone, also known as a baking stone, is a rectangular piece of stoneware designed to mimic the baking surface of a hearth oven. The desired lift in baking bread is difficult to achieve without one, but it is not essential in the same way that bread flour is not absolutely necessary to make bread. It is placed directly on the wire rack in the oven, and can also be stored there. The stone takes time to fully charge with heat, and therefore needs at least 1 hour of preheating to attain the proper temperature. An inexpensive alternative is to fill a sheet pan or line the oven rack with unglazed quarry tiles, available at tile stores and some home centres.

Baking on the hot surface of a baking stone encourages lift in the bread known as *oven spring*. The same effect cannot take place if the bread is baked on a sheet pan, even if the sheet pan is preheated along with the oven. The baking stone is thicker and retains more heat, allowing for a constant release of this energy during the bake. Metal, on the other hand, is much more conductive, and the heat quickly dissipates into the surface of the dough, resulting in a short-lived boost.

### SERRATED KNIFE

The crumb structure reveals much about the bread, and slicing the bread using a sharp, serrated bread knife is the best way to ensure little or no damage to the crumb inside.

### LAME

The baker's lame is used for scoring the cuts in the bread just before baking, creating tension-release points that help control the final shape of the bread. The razor-sharp edges are good for about 100 cuts, and I always recommend purchasing a lame with the option of replacing the blades. If you do not have a lame, using a single-edge razor or a craft knife; a very sharp serrated

A lame cutting the dough

A wooden peel

knife can work, too. A lame is to the baker as a paintbrush is to the artist; it allows the baker to "sign" bread with a signature scoring technique.

## PARCHMENT PAPER

Parchment paper has many uses in the kitchen, but its primary use in baking is to prevent sticking and ensure a quick and easy cleanup. It is available in half–sheet pan size (13 x 18 inches [33 x 46 cm]) as well as on a roll and can be either white (bleached) or natural (unbleached).

## PASTRY BRUSHES

Pastry brushes are used to spread oils, washes, and glazes onto the dough. Inexpensive brushes with very soft bristles purchased at art stores can replace anything from a kitchen supply store. The soft bristles are very gentle and do not damage the most delicate laminated layers of even a croissant (see page 134).

## PEEL

A peel is a wooden board with a handle designed to load bread in and out of the oven. Any shape will do, as long as it fits into the oven and can

accommodate the shape and size of the bread. As an alternative, use a sheet pan turned upside down and lined with parchment paper (see page 41).

## PLASTIC PROOFING TUBS

Plastic containers are preferred because they assume a neutral temperature, which allows for consistent fermentation. Regular plastic food storage containers work fine if they are big enough. If choosing to invest in special proofing tubs, do not forget the lids, and look for containers that have few or no ridges on the bottom. Dough tends to stick in these ridges, making them more difficult to clean.

An assortment of proofing containers and lids

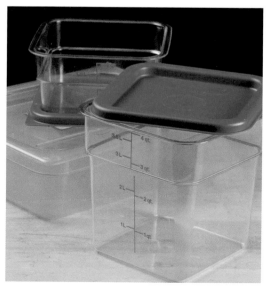

## PROOFING BOARD

A proofing board is a flat, rectangular board made of wood or plywood with an industry standard size of approximately 18 x 26 inches (46 x 65 cm). These boards function as portable surfaces to hold resting dough. In a bakeshop, the dough is placed on the boards that are then moved to be stored in vertical racks, minimizing the amount of space needed. For the home kitchen, the size is not critical and any large wooden cutting board will suffice.

## SHEET PAN

The simplest choice is a single-layer, heavy-gauge aluminum sheet pan with a lip. Most residential ovens can only accommodate half-size sheet pans that measure about 13 x 18 inches (33 x 46 cm). Invest in good-quality sheet pans and they will more than likely outlast the oven.

A loaf pan filled with metal and preheated with the oven is a good steam generator.

## STEAM TRAY

Professional bread ovens have a steam injection function that produces bursts of steam inside the oven. This humidity allows the outer crust of the dough to expand to its fullest potential before its final shape is captured in the baking. To replicate this function, a loaf pan three-quarters filled with metal (such as metal pie weights or clean, miscellaneous hardware), lava rocks, or ceramic briquettes (used in some gas barbecue grills) is placed next to the oven wall and preheated along with the oven. Just before baking, lay a water-soaked facecloth or some ice cubes in the pan and listen to that generator hiss—just be sure to protect yourself from the resulting steam!

## THERMOMETER AND TIMER

Many digital thermometers also have a timing mode. This tool is indispensable; it takes the guesswork out of determining the temperature of the water for the pre-ferments and final doughs and the temperature of the dough as it comes off the mixer, as well as timing the fermentation and baking cycles. Try to get a model that has a long cord from the unit to the temperature probe. Analog probe thermometers are fine to use, but infrared thermometers have their limitations, as they can only measure the temperature on the surface of the dough.

A probe thermometer with a timing function

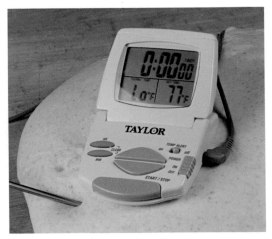

# Philosophy of Baking:
# CULTIVATING A LOVE FOR LEARNING

One sure route to mastering the art of baking is continuing education. Since I am a teacher, I confess I am biased toward this route. But as a teacher, I know that learning is truly continuous—it never, ever stops. I constantly acquire new information and insights about bread from my colleagues and baking friends, even from my own students.

By reading this book, you have already taken the initiative to educate yourself. Every baker has a slightly different way of baking and presents

material in a tailored manner. Your obligation is to feed your own unique learning style. Inform and challenge yourself. Experiment with formulas, with flours. Read another book, or three. Peruse culinary magazines. Visit a new bakery (and sample their offerings). Spend some quality time online. Read a blog whose style appeals to you. Travel, explore, and taste.

I highly recommend taking hands-on classes in bread baking with an experienced baker, or even attending a demonstration. Nothing can take the place of seeing and feeling the dough in action firsthand. The Bread Bakers Guild of America and other international associations are wonderful organisations whose mission is to promote the advancement and education of handmade bread baking. Their websites list sponsored workshops and links to international culinary schools and educational opportunities.

Bakers tend to be a friendly bunch (though again, I may be biased) and are very generous with their time. Most will happily answer questions about their craft, so don't be afraid to ask. If you live near a bakery, visit it often—and make friends with the proprietors. An experienced baker is a great mentor.

# Ovens

There are four main types of ovens: conventional, convection, combination, and wood fired. *Conventional ovens* have been the workhorses in most residential households for many years and are heated through top or bottom electric or gas-fired elements. A *convection oven* uses a fan to force the hot air around inside the oven to provide a more even distribution of the heat, cooking the food more quickly in less time. A *combination oven* is a conventional oven with a convection mode, and a *wood-fired oven* is a masonry oven designed and built to capture and utilize the heat and energy produced through a wood fire.

Each oven type has certain qualities, and it is best to just learn to adapt to the one you have and make it work for you. A conventional oven, for example, is great for baking lean doughs, like ciabatta or baguette, with a few modifications. First, a baking stone must be in place in the lower third section of the oven, and second, a steaming tray must be utilized. (See the baguette formula, pages 58–64, for more on using steam.) Using a convection oven or a convection mode promotes more even browning, but the hot forced air tends to dry out the product. This is not ideal for handmade lean doughs, but it is a great system for baking cookies as well as breads made from enriched doughs, like brioche and challah. *Note: Due to the intensity of the heat forced directly onto the product, the temperature in a convection oven is set 20°F to 40°F (10°C to 20°C) lower than a regular conventional oven.*

Using a peel to transfer loaves into the oven

With the rising interest in hearth baking and cooking coupled with the trend of outdoor kitchen spaces, wood-fired ovens have grown more popular and available in recent years. They can be constructed with the traditional brick method or even out of mud, but a manufactured oven core specially engineered for this purpose can simplify the building process immensely. The heat source in these ovens is wood alone, making it extremely challenging to control the temperature. However, once mastered, there is nothing quite as magical as baking bread in a wood-fired oven!

## MOVING BREAD FROM COUNTER TO OVEN

There are a few simple methods for moving bread from the counter (or preparation area) into the oven, and from oven to counter once the bread has baked.

### Using a Peel

Sprinkle the peel generously with cornmeal or rice flour, which acts like tiny ball bearings for the dough to glide on. Place the dough onto the peel. Hold the peel level to the baking stone and position the loaf in the approximate place where it will bake. Then angle the peel down and pull it straight back without too much hesitation, leaving the loaf on the stone (much like the old trick of pulling a tablecloth out from under the dishes).

To remove a baked loaf from the oven, simply slide the peel underneath it and remove it from the oven, or just remove the loaf with oven mitts.

### Using a Sheet Pan

Turn a sheet pan upside down and place a piece of parchment paper on the bottom. Place the dough onto the parchment paper. Slide the entire sheet of parchment and bread directly onto the stone.

To remove from the oven, pull the parchment paper back onto a sheet pan and out of the oven, or just remove the loaf with oven mitts.

The sheet pan method of transferring loaves into the oven

# Pre-Ferment Basics

A pre-ferment is a portion of dough that is mixed together prior to preparing the final dough. The pre-ferment is allowed to ferment in a controlled manner before being added to the final dough. The many benefits of pre-ferments make it a good investment of the time it takes to prepare and incorporate them into the final dough, including increased flavour, strength, and shelf life. Naturally leavened pre-ferments known as starters are used solely in sourdough breads.

All other breads are made with store-bought (or commercially manufactured) yeast, and their pre-ferments are commercially leavened as well. Starters need constant attention and feeding to ensure consistent leavening activity. Commercially leavened pre-ferments are prepared and used up all at once; these are the types of pre-ferments used in this book.

Pre-ferments can be stored either at room temperature or in the refrigerator, each manner of storage lending a very specific characteristic to the flavour profile of the final product. Cold-stored pre-ferments assume an acidic flavour profile, comparable to lemon juice or vinegar. Pre-ferments stored at room temperature have a lactic flavour profile, comparable to yogurt.

## PRE-FERMENTS LEAVENED WITH MANUFACTURED YEAST

There are four main types of commercially leavened pre-ferments:

### Poolish

A poolish is the wettest pre-ferment, with a one-to-one ratio of flour to water. It adds a sweet, nutty, and slightly lactic flavour profile, ideal for breads such as the baguette (see page 58).

Mix a poolish a day before baking by placing the water in the bowl first, followed by the flour and yeast. Mix it with a spatula to a nice smooth consistency. Put it into a plastic container that will allow for the poolish to expand to twice its size and cover with a lid. A perfectly matured poolish has a good balance of large air bubbles and smaller impressions on the top surface. A poolish should not be kept for more than 24 hours. If a "high water mark" is visible on the side of the container, it indicates that the poolish has overfermented and can no longer contribute properly to the fermentation process.

An example of a smooth, correctly mixed poolish (right) and one that has been incorrectly mixed (left)

### Biga

This pre-ferment is firmer than the poolish. It was originally developed in Italy to help strengthen the lower gluten-forming flours traditional to that region. It has an acidic profile along with ample strength-building characteristics, making it a good pre-ferment for products such as pane francese (see page 86).

Although a biga can be mixed by hand, a stand mixer usually does the job better and faster. Make sure there are no dry spots in the dough and that it comes together as a smooth mass. Coat a plastic container with some nonstick cooking spray. Place the biga upside down in the container and then turn it over so that the top is coated with oil. This allows the biga to expand without cracking. Place a lid on the container and allow it to ferment typically at room temperature. A perfectly matured biga will double in size and, if a piece is torn off, small air cells are visible. A strong fermented odor is also present.

### Sponge

A sponge pre-ferment was originally used to produce pan breads. It has a hydration rate of 60 to 63 percent and is often used in enriched doughs. A sponge does not contain any sugar or fats and gives the yeast a chance to jump-start the fermentation process and strengthen before being added to the final dough. Fats and sugars have a tenderizing effect on dough, and so the extra strength imparted from the sponge is a welcome addition to the final dough. A sponge is mixed and handled the same way as a biga.

### Pâte Fermentée (Old Dough)

This type of pre-ferment is a piece of fully fermented and developed dough that is saved from one batch and added to a new batch the following day. After a dough is mixed and allowed to go through its bulk fermentation, some of it is removed, placed in a container, covered, and refrigerated overnight. The next day, this pre-ferment is added to the final dough after the cleanup stage. This is the only type of pre-ferment that has been mixed into a full gluten development. It adds strength to the dough and imparts an acidic flavour due to its cold storage. Unless the same bread is made every day at home, the *pâte fermentée* is a difficult pre-ferment to utilize on a regular basis. Bakeries with fixed production schedules can easily take advantage of this pre-ferment.

A smooth, correctly mixed biga on the right and an incorrectly mixed biga with dry spots on the left. (These images also represent correctly and incorrectly mixed sponges.)

# Shaping Basics

Each bakery may have its own way of shaping any type of bread; many different shaping techniques can achieve the same style of bread. The journey the dough takes is as individual as the baker himself.

## PRESHAPING

The first stage of shaping, known as preshaping, occurs after bulk fermentation. The baker divides the dough into small portions and, using his hands, aligns the gluten matrix into its desired shape. How a baker handles the dough at this point will have a direct effect on the final product. If the dough is handled too roughly, then the interior crumb structure will become tight. Handling the dough loosely allows some form corrections to be made in the final shaping, if necessary.

Wooden surfaces have a nice warmth and just enough texture to give the dough some traction during shaping. If the dough is too sticky, flour may be judiciously sprinkled on the work surface to help prevent it from sticking.

If the final shape is rectangular or has sides (such as a panned loaf or a baguette), then the dough should be preshaped into a roll (log). If the final shape is round (such as a *miche* or *boule*), then the dough should be preshaped into a round.

### Preshaping a Round

Take a portion of dough and gently cup your hand (or hands, depending on the size) over it with your fingers relaxed and draped over the dough. Using a small circular motion, move the dough around on the surface so that it starts to assume a ball-like shape. As you move the dough, gently push the heel of your hand into the dough as you circle away from you and then use your fingers to bring the dough back toward you. Continue this until the dough starts to feel tight.

### Preshaping a Log

Take a unit of dough that is fairly rectangular in form and place your hands under the edge farthest from you. Gently roll up the dough toward your body, much like rolling up a sleeping bag. Any large air pockets will be expelled and the gluten structure will start to tighten up to bring some direction to the piece.

After preshaping rounds or logs, place seam side down on a surface (preferably wood) and cover with a couche or plastic during the resting phase.

## FINAL SHAPING

This is the stage at which the baker establishes the final shape of the bread. During this process, consistency in shape and size is the goal. Take the preshaped dough and invert it so that the seam side is up. With flat hands, gently press down to start to expel any large air pockets, evenly distributing the air cells throughout the piece. Do not completely flatten the dough. If the dough is too sticky to handle, sprinkle flour on the work surface as you coax the dough into its final shape. But be careful not to overdo it; heavily dusting with flour can quickly add up to enough flour to change the outcome of the final product.

Preshaped logs (left) and rounds (right)

## Boule or Round Loaf

Start with a preshaped round with the seam side up and gently press down on it to expel the gases. With your hand, take a point on the edge of the dough and bring it in toward the centre. Keep repeating this process, moving around the perimeter of the dough, creating overlapping pleats of dough. (Imagine bending daisy petals to the centre of the flower.) Once complete, turn the dough over so that the pleats are on the bottom.

Now repeat a motion from the preshaping round: With the edges of your hands on the table, cup your hands around the back of the dough and move the dough forward and clockwise. The surface of the dough will begin to tighten as the front edge of the dough creeps underneath itself. Reposition your hands and repeat the motion until the loaf has a nice, smooth surface. Place the dough in a couched bowl or basket with the seam side up for the final proofing stage.

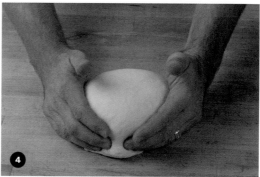

Shaping a boule or round

## Bâtard or Oval Loaf

As with a boule, start with a preshaped round with the seam side up and gently press down on it to expel the gases. Take the far edge of the dough and coax it with your hands toward you. Press into the centre of the dough, keeping your thumbs horizontally aligned, and apply a down-and-back motion with your thumbs. It is almost as if you are rolling the dough onto the thumbs and then back away. Repeat a few times and then fold up the tips of the short ends of the dough toward the centre. Again, coax the far edge of the dough toward you, rolling the dough so that the seams and folds are eventually at the bottom. Gently rock the dough back and forth to help tighten the seam on the bottom and finish by compressing the ends so that the loaf attains a football-like shape. Place the dough seam side up onto a couche and allow it to final proof. If the dough tends to lose its shape, try increasing the amount of back-to-front folds during the shaping stage.

Shaping a bâtard or oval

## Baguette or Long Loaf

A traditional French baguette is too long to fit into a regular oven, and so the classic characteristics of a long, thin baguette have been adapted for the home by way of the "mini baguette." They are shaped in the same manner, just not with the same amount of dough. Because the shaping process is rather long, complicated, and unique to the baguette, it is described in its entirety in the baguette formula (see pages 58–64).

Keep in mind that though the form of the baguette is simple, the shaping of one is anything but. It takes the hands hours of choreography to manipulate and coax the dough into the elegant, iconic shape. Each part of the hand, from the heel to the thumb, plays a role. Some motions require a lighter, gentler touch, while others require more force and pressure. As you practice shaping baguettes, pay attention to these differences and notice how the dough reacts to your touch.

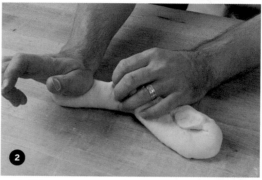

The beginning stages of shaping a mini baguette

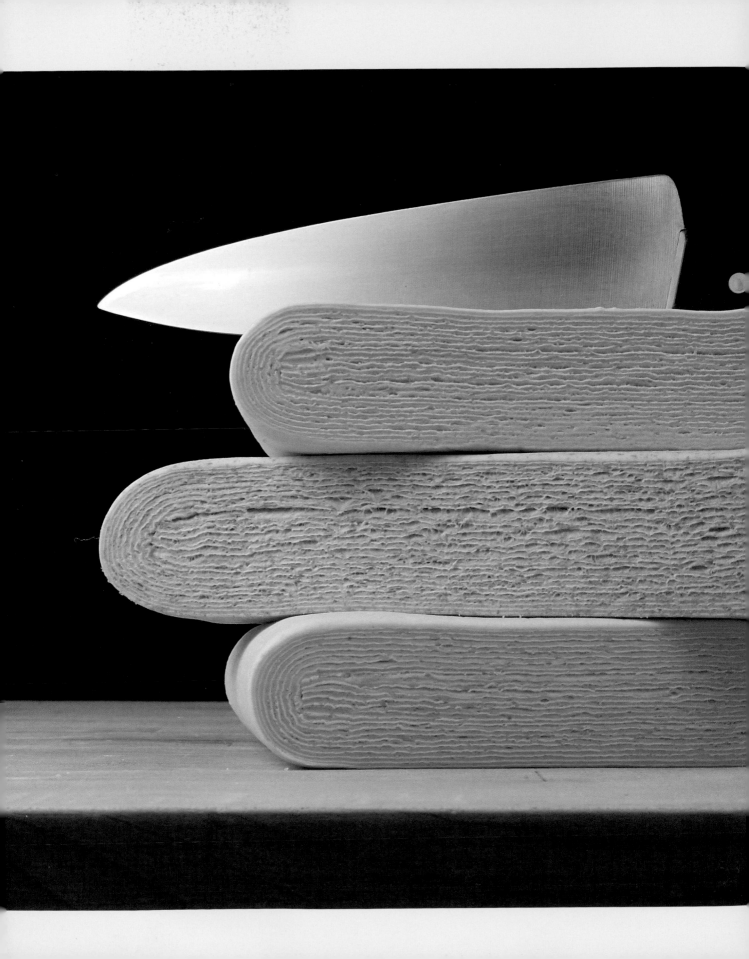

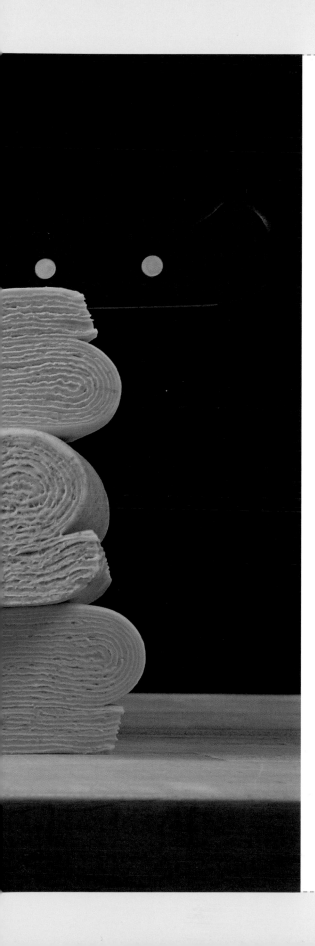

# PART TWO

# Baking

NOW FOR THE FUN PART! There is nothing quite like the aroma of bread baking permeating the air, beckoning to all those lucky enough to be nearby. Armed with the basics, it is time to roll up your sleeves and get your hands on some dough. The process of baking is a complete delight, touching each of the senses in its own unique way. As you bake, you will gain experience and confidence and develop your own style of dancing with the dough.

It is helpful to have a fundamental understanding of the phases of baking, and an overview of this information is succinctly presented so you can grasp the concepts quickly. The formulas and their many variations are only pages away, which means that freshly baked bread is not too far behind!

# CHAPTER THREE

# The Ten Steps of Baking

THE PROFESSIONS OF BAKER and architect have astonishing parallels. Both use simple materials as the building blocks for something seemingly complex. For the architect, it is wood, steel, brick, and stone, but for the baker, the materials are flour, yeast, water, and salt. A good architect carefully drafts the minutiae of his plans, accounting for each detail's relation to the whole. Instead of an architectural plan, a baker has a recipe formula. The frame is erected, and each step of the construction process relies on the previous one. A baker has his mixing, kneading, rising, and baking. Each component is equally integral to the success of the project, or the edible loaf.

The biggest difference, of course, is that the building has both a structural and visual integrity designed to last for years. Bread has a comparatively short life span, more like a blink, and is best enjoyed when it is fresh.

All bread-making formulas follow a set sequence of definitive stages. In this chapter, these stages are sorted into ten basic steps and introduced at length. These same ten stages are employed in each of the formulas in this book.

1. Mise en Place
2. Mixing
3. Fermentation
4. Stretch and Folds/Degassing
5. Dividing
6. Preshaping/Shaping
7. Final Proof/Panning
8. Scoring
9. Baking
10. Cooling/Storage

It is possible to follow a recipe and bake decent bread without a thorough understanding of these stages. My own constant quest for knowledge has pushed me to explore the boundaries of baking, and I think it is critical to know what is happening at each step of the process and why. It takes years of baking experience to develop an intuitive reading of the dough, but becoming familiar with the concepts of the ten steps of baking will illuminate the baking process, from mixing to kneading and beyond.

Mise en Place

Mixing

### STEP ONE:
# Mise en Place

The French term *mise en place* literally means "setting in place" and is the primary organisational philosophy across all culinary fields worldwide. It is about preparing both mentally and physically for the task at hand. Essentially it requires reading through the formula in its entirety, gathering the necessary equipment, and scaling (or measuring) the ingredients. All of the main formulas in this book start with mise en place. In addition to the basic equipment necessary for all formulas (listed in chapter 2, page 23), a list of special equipment required to make each bread is provided alongside the formula.

### STEP TWO:
# Mixing

Mixing is the stage at which the ingredients are combined and married into a common mass. It can be done by hand, in a food processor, or in a mixer. The first mixing speed is a low speed in order to combine all of the ingredients in a uniform manner. This initial mix does not take very long, maybe 3 or 4 minutes, and very little gluten is developed during this time. The consistency of the dough is pastelike with little strength, but it is critical that the ingredients be mixed slowly at first to ensure their complete incorporation with each other. The second mix increases the mixing speed and encourages the formation of more gluten strands. Strength is built and oxygen is incorporated into the dough through the action of mixing. A certain amount of strength and oxygen is necessary, but when continued unchecked, the oxygen creates a whiter dough with a tighter, denser crumb structure, a trait that bakers try to avoid like the plague.

### STEP THREE:
# Fermentation

After all ingredients have been incorporated and the dough has been mixed to the baker's satisfaction, it is removed from the mixer and the fermentation stage begins. With regard to taste, this is one of the most important steps in the process, as 75 percent of the flavour of the bread is developed during this time. The dough has taken quite a beating in the mixer, and it is time to let it recover, relax, and ferment. It is placed in a neutral environment with the ideal temperature between 75°F and 78°F (24°C to 26°C) and rests in this stage anywhere from 1½ to 3 hours. The duration of this initial resting period is known to bakers as the *bulk fermentation*.

## STEP FOUR:
# Stretch and Folds/Degassing

Starting about halfway into the bulk fermentation process, many doughs benefit from a series of stretches and folds. A complete sequence of this technique is illustrated in chapter 2 (page 32). With this hand manipulation, a baker is able to assess the dough's development through the sense of touch. A stretch and fold also performs three key functions. First, it degasses the dough and expels the old carbon dioxide, making room for the yeast's continuous production of new carbon dioxide. Second, it creates strength by aligning the gluten strands in a controlled formation. And third, it equalizes the temperature of the dough by folding and redistributing the cooler sections of the dough into the warmer ones.

## STEP FIVE:
# Dividing

One batch of dough usually yields more than one loaf of bread. The main dough is divided into smaller units for shaping and baking. Using a scale is helpful in ensuring uniform pieces. After the bulk fermentation, the dough is turned onto a clean and lightly floured work surface and divided into segments with a dough divider or bench scraper. The dough should be cut cleanly, not torn or ripped. Smaller pieces of dough are added or subtracted to attain the desired weight, although a singular piece is most ideal. Accurate dividing helps during the baking process—if all units are uniform to begin with, chances are they will bake in a uniform manner as well.

Fermentation

Stretch and Folds/Degassing

Dividing

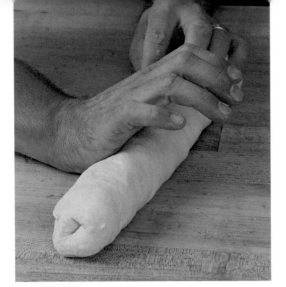

Preshaping/Shaping

Final Proof/Panning

Scoring

## STEP SIX:
# Preshaping/Shaping

Preshaping the dough is how the baker starts to coax the dough into a certain shape. The gluten matrix is trained to assume a particular form and to retain it. The final shape of the dough is always considered during the preshaping process. (See pages 44–47 for more on preshaping and shaping doughs.)

Care should be taken not to add too much flour during this preshaping process, and the action should be kept loose. There is usually a resting period of 20 to 30 minutes between preshaping and shaping, which gives the dough time to relax and remember what it was just taught. The first unit to be pre-shaped is always the first unit to be shaped. The final shaping of the dough should be done consistently to ensure an even and balanced product.

## STEP SEVEN:
# Final Proof/Panning

This stage gives the dough its final rise. The ideal situation for proofing is a protected environment (no drafts) at 75°F to 78°F (24°C to 26°C). The dough is still fermenting, yet at a slower rate than during the first and "official" fermentation stage. Taking advantage of this, the baker pushes the volume of the loaf to approximately 85 percent of its full capacity.

Judging the extent of a proof is a skill learned over time; even experienced bakers find it tricky to do on sight alone. A good test: make an impression in the dough with a finger; the dough should slowly push back, but it does not completely recover its original shape. A valuable exercise for a beginner is to mix a batch of dough, shape it, and observe the complete proofing process until the dough collapses. Touching the dough at different stages of the proof will inform your senses of what to look for during the proofing cycle.

## STEP EIGHT:
# Scoring

The scoring of bread may appear to be purely decorative, but it serves an essential purpose: It steers the last moment of expansion during baking, and consequently the final shape of the bread. When the surface of a bread is cut, a weak spot in the loaf is created. Just as lightning seeks the shortest path to the ground, expansion energy in bread seeks out the weakest point in the surface. By scoring the bread, the baker directs this energy. A dough sliced at precisely the right angle and at a precise depth will result in a beautiful transition between crust and crumb; the energy release is perfectly channeled, creating lift.

This step does not apply to every bread formula in this book. For example, a brioche that is gently formed and correctly proofed does not require any cuts for a perfect finish.

### STEP NINE:
# Baking

A great deal of care and time has been invested to get the dough to this point, and it can be nerve-racking to place the dough in the oven. This is, after all, the final, dramatic test of a baker. As the dough comes in contact with the hot baking stone, the intense, direct heat seals the bottom of the bread and drives the energy toward the top, creating oven spring. As baking progresses, water in the bread evaporates and the starches congeal and solidify. The sugars start to caramelize on the exterior, forming the crust and introducing a completely new flavour profile to the bread.

Baking

### STEP TEN:
# Cooling/Storage

Sometimes overlooked as a true step, cooling is essential to the baking process. In France, bread is required to cool for a minimum amount of time before becoming available for sale. In truth, the bread is not completely finished when it comes out of the oven. After the bread is placed on a cooling rack, the starches continue to gelatinize, setting the bread into its final form and flavour. As tempting as sampling the piping-hot loaf may be, patience and restraint should be observed; the subtle nuances of a bread's flavour can only fully be appreciated in a cooled state. (Even the most seasoned of bakers need to remind themselves of this from time to time!)

After cooling, bread can be stored, cut side down, on a cutting board. If it needs to be stored longer than the day it was baked, place the bread in a paper bag. Breads made with enriched dough, such as pain de mie (see page 106) and brioche (see page 124), can be wrapped in plastic. If the bread will be frozen, it can be wrapped in plastic wrap.

Cooling/Storage

# CHAPTER FOUR

# The Bread Formulas

ONE OF THE MOST innovative bakeries I've ever visited was a tiny shop in Bavaria. I gazed at their display window, and their more than forty breads, and was confounded: How could a shop this small in size produce such a variety? Intrigued, I entered the store, introduced myself, and asked to speak to the head baker, who graciously brought me back into the bakeshop to explain its operation.

All their breads were made from *five* formulas. A large batch of each formula was divided into smaller batches. To each small batch, a different ingredient—from olives to nuts to dried fruit—was introduced. This production-oriented insight was a revelation.

With the following ten formulas, this innovative streamlined style of baking is possible for the home baker. Each formula features unique flavour variations to experiment with. These are tried-and-true professional formulas that experienced bakers as well as avid home bakers have enjoyed with great success.

## USING THE FORMULAS

These formulas are presented according to the Ten Steps of Baking (see pages 50–55) and do not follow a traditional recipe layout. This invites you into each of the dough's phases. In the appendix, each formula has a preparation timeline, to help estimate the overall work involved. The times given are generalized and should not be substituted for actual formula instructions.

The dough preparation and shaping and baking of all formulas have difficulty ratings: easy, medium, and difficult. Starting with an easier formula, such as Pane Francese (page 86) or Pizza (page 92), will whet the appetite for baking while developing the techniques and confidence for the more challenging formulas.

Each formula (and formula variation) lists special equipment needed in addition to the basic mise en place equipment and tools listed in chapter 2 (page 23). Ideal water temperatures are specified in the formulas; deviations from these temperatures can be accommodated through shortening (if warmer) or lengthening (if cooler) the fermentation times. Also, if you are a professional baker or a serious home baker who likes to work with baker's percentages (see page 165), they are listed in each formula. So turn the page and let's begin!

| DOUGH PREPARATION: | **Medium** |
| SHAPING AND BAKING: | **Difficult** |
| YIELD: | **Makes 4 baguettes, 14 inches (35 cm) each** |
| TOTAL TIME: | **Approximately 4 hours and 15 minutes over 2 days** |

# FORMULA ONE: Baguette Dough

A BEAUTIFUL BAGUETTE is truly a baker's masterpiece. The deep, golden crust creates a miniature mountain landscape, complete with peaks and ravines. Inside, the creamy, open crumb reveals little cups just the right size for holding butter or jam. It is, quite simply, the perfect loaf of bread.

The baguette is a standard measure of skill of a baker: Despite its simple ingredients, it is one of the most difficult breads to bake successfully and consistently. If you are a beginning baker, you may want to start off with a more forgiving dough formula, such as the Pane Francese (page 86), before attempting the baguette. However, even a determined beginner with a little experience can produce wonderful bread using the easier-to-shape épi, scroll, and breadstick variations. And always remember, practice makes perfect.

## POOLISH

| Ingredient | Metric | Weight | Volume | Baker's % |
|---|---|---|---|---|
| Bread flour | 200 g | 7 oz | | 100 |
| Water, 77°F (25°C) | 200 g | 7 oz | 210 ml | 100 |
| Instant yeast | Pinch | Pinch | Pinch | 0.1 |

Prepare the poolish the night before baking. Combine the bread flour, water, and yeast and mix until smooth. Cover the bowl with plastic wrap and let stand at room temperature (68°F to 70°F [20°C to 21°C]) for 12 to 16 hours overnight.

## FINAL DOUGH

| Ingredient | Metric | Weight | Volume | Baker's % |
|---|---|---|---|---|
| Bread flour | 400 g | 14.1 oz | | 100 |
| Water, 92°F (33°C) | 200 g | 7 oz | 210 ml | 50 |
| Instant yeast | 1.5 g | 0.05 oz | ¾ tsp | 0.38 |
| Salt | 12 g | 0.4 oz | 2 tsp | 3 |
| Diastatic malt* (optional) | 4 g | 0.14 oz | 1½ tsp | 1 |
| Poolish | All of it | All of it | All of it | 100 |

*See page 61

2. Baguette dough after mixing

3. After mixing the dough, pour it into the prepared container.

## 1. Mise en Place

Prepare and scale all ingredients.

**ADDITIONAL SPECIAL EQUIPMENT**
Baking stone
Couche
Proofing board
Transfer board
Peel
Flour sifter
Razor or lame
Steaming pan or water spray bottle

## 2. Mixing

Using a 5-quart (5 L) stand mixer with a dough hook attachment, combine the bread flour, water, instant yeast, salt, diastatic malt, and poolish on low speed for approximately 4 minutes.

When the ingredients start to come together into the cleanup stage (see page 31), increase the mixer's speed to medium and continue to mix for 2 to 3 minutes. All ingredients should be completely blended and the dough should have a uniform consistency.

## 3. Fermentation

Gently pour the dough into a plastic container whose interior has been coated with nonstick cooking spray. The container should be large enough to accommodate the dough mass to at least double in size and should have a lid. Check the temperature of the dough with a thermometer probe; it should be between 75°F and 78°F (24°C and 26°C).

Cover with the plastic lid and let the dough rest for 45 minutes. If a lid is unavailable, plastic wrap may be used, although it should not come into contact with the dough.

## 4. Stretch and Folds/Degassing

After the dough has rested, perform one series of stretch and folds (see page 32) on the dough.

Allow dough to rest for another 45 minutes.

## 5. Dividing

Invert the container onto a lightly floured table and allow gravity to release the dough from the container. Do not

## The Use of MALT

Diastatic malt is used by many professional bakers and comes in both a powder and liquid form. It is made from sprouted grains (usually barley) that have been dried and ground and contains natural enzymes. When diastatic malt is used as an ingredient in bread dough, these enzymes help to break down the starch to make sugars. The sugars are by-products of this breakdown process and serve two functions. First, they provide food for the yeast. If the yeast has enough food, it grows actively during the fermentation process. More fermentation equals better rise and flavour. Second, the sugars caramelize during the baking process and help to build a nice crispy brown crust. Not only does this make the bread visually appealing, it also improves its shelf life and helps the bread stay fresher longer. To simplify, the malt aids the dough much like a sports drink aids an athlete. It improves the performance but is not absolutely necessary. Because most flours have a small percentage of malt added to them, this additional boost of malt is a personal choice and considered an optional ingredient.

scrape or bang out the dough, since every extra movement toughens the dough and creates a tighter crumb structure.

Using a scale and a dough divider, divide the dough into four (8.8-ounce) 250-gram rectangular portions. Distribute any extra dough equally among the pieces.

Preheat oven with baking stone in place to 475°F (240°C, gas mark 9). Place loaf pan for steaming in the oven while preheating (see Steam Tray, page 38).

### 6. Preshaping/Shaping

Working on a lightly floured surface, degas the dough by gently patting down the rectangle. Begin to roll the short edge toward the centre. Continue a winding motion from the back to the front until a stubby log shape is formed. The dough should have a light and airy quality.

5. The dough is accurately divided using a scale.

6a. Preshaping the baguette dough into logs

6b. The preshaped dough is placed on a board to rest.

6c. Degas the dough with gentle but firm downward pressure.

Place the dough seam side down onto a couche or proofing board cover, and let rest for 20 to 30 minutes.

Take the dough and place it on a table, seam side up, and use gentle but firm downward pressure to degas the dough. Do not try to flatten it; rather just even out the consistency of the dough. Proper degassing results in even distribution of the air cells, making it easier to roll out the baguettes.

Roll up the long end of the dough with the same rolling motion used for preshaping (see step 6, page 54).

With the heel of the hand, and working from one end of the baguette to the other, compress the seam into the main body of the dough, sealing them together. Do not compress the ends of the baguette at this point.

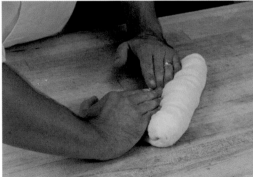

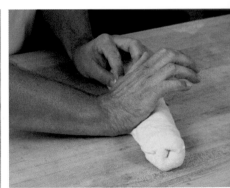

6d. Rolling up the baguette dough is part of the final shaping.

6e. Seal the baguette seam using the heel of the hand.

6f. Roll the baguettes using a constant and even pressure.

With the hands angled slightly inward and overlapping at the centre, begin to roll out the baguette, using a constant downward rolling motion. Extend the dough so it is approximately 14 inches (35 cm) long. Apply even and symmetrical pressure when rolling. Compress the ends of the baguette only when they are at the final length .

7. Carefully lay the baguettes onto the pleated couche.

## OPTIONAL: Dusting with Rice Flour

If desired, lightly dust the tops of the baguettes with bread or rice flour. Because rice flour browns at a higher temperature than wheat flour, it remains lighter during baking. This decorative contrast between the crust and the cuts gives the baguette a distinctive look. Note: This technique is not allowed in France, where by law the ingredients of a baguette are solely restricted to white flour, water, salt, and yeast.

### 7. Final Proof/Panning

Place the baguettes seam side down on a lightly flour-dusted couche. Fold the couche between each baguette, forming a pleated ridge. The pleated ridge supports the baguette as it continues to proof while still allowing room for expansion..

Cover the baguettes with the couche. Lay plastic wrap over the entire couche to prevent the baguettes from drying out. Let rest for a final proofing stage for 45 to 60 minutes.

8a. Transferring the baguette from the couche to the peel

### 8. Scoring

Transfer to a board by gently rolling the dough off the couche and onto the board. The seam of the baguette will be up. Roll back onto a lightly flour-dusted peel or parchment-lined sheet pan. Now the seam will be down again. Using a board to transfer keeps the baguette nice and straight.

With a single-edged razor or a baker's lame, use a quick, decisive motion to slice the scores on the top of the bread. These cuts will run lengthwise, not side to side, at a slight angle and will overlap each other by one-third of the previous cut (see [age 62]. For a 14-inch (35 cm) baguette-style bread, the recommended number of cuts is 3 or 5.

8b. Cutting the scores into the baguette using a baker's lame

## 9. Baking

Before the baguettes are placed in the oven, soak a piece of towel (or facecloth) with water for the loaf pan steamer.

Transfer the baguettes into the oven using either the peel or sheet-pan method (see page 41).

Place the water-soaked towel into the steamer pan, ensuring the towel is completely contained in the pan. This creates a burst of steam in the oven, so wear oven gloves and be prepared to move your hands! Close the oven door quickly to prevent the steam from escaping. (Alternatively, use the water spray bottle method described below.)

When the baguettes attain a golden colour, open oven door one or two times to allow excess steam to escape. (The extra humidity helped create the crust and should be released from the oven.) Continue baking for a minimum of 20 minutes total. Prop the oven door open with a wooden spoon for the last 2 minutes of baking.

## 10. Cooling/Storing

When the baguettes have finished baking, remove them from the oven and place on a wire rack to cool.

Allow the baguettes to cool for at least 30 minutes. Baguettes stale very quickly, so freeze any bread that is not eaten the same day. Wrap the baguettes tightly in plastic and place in the freezer, where they can be stored for up to 2 weeks.

## CREATING STEAM in the Oven

Some recipes require steam be created in the oven during baking. To prepare for this step, fill a loaf pan halfway with small metal pieces (see Steam Tray, page 38). Place next to the oven wall on the baking stone (or rack). It can also be placed in the bottom of the oven, although it will be harder to reach when the oven is hot. This will act as the steamer during baking. It should be preheated along with the oven.

Alternatively, a water spray bottle can also be used to create steam. When needed, spray the water onto the oven walls and immediately close the oven door.

## VARIATION: Épi

SHAPING AND BAKING: **Medium**

YIELD: **4 épis, 14 inches (35 cm) each**

THIS ÉPI VARIATION (short for *épi de blé,* meaning "sheaf of wheat") uses the baguette dough to create a stunning bread that is surprisingly easy to make. The final shape resembles a wheat shaft, and the "kernels" break off with ease, making it a perfect bread to serve when guests come for dinner.

**Prepare Formula One (Baguette Dough) through step 7, Final Proof/Panning.** (See pages 58–62).

> **ADDITIONAL SPECIAL EQUIPMENT**
> Scissors

### 8. Scoring

Instead of scoring, scissor cuts release the tension in this variation. Place the baguette on the peel. Hold a pair of scissors at a 30° angle and, starting one end of the baguette, cut three-quarters of the way through the baguette.

Move this "kernel" to one side of the loaf. Make the next cut about 1½ inches (4 cm) from the first cut and place this kernel to the opposite side of the loaf.

Continue cutting the length of the loaf, alternating the kernels from side to side.

8. Move each kernel of the épi immediately after cutting.

### 9. Baking

Transfer into oven, steam, and bake following the directions for a baguette (page 64). The shape of an épi is more fragile than a regular baguette, so extra care should be taken during transfer.

### 10. Cooling/Storage

Due to their slightly fragile shape, cool the épis on a wire rack completely before enjoying. They are best enjoyed immediately or shared with friends or family, as storing épis for more than a day is tricky.

## The Seeded ÉPI

A assortment of *épis* can be made by adding seeds to the crusts. Before cutting the kernels, spray the surface of the épis with a little water and lightly roll them in poppy, sesame, or other type of seeds. (The same technique works with the original baguette as well, although scoring will be more of a challenge.)

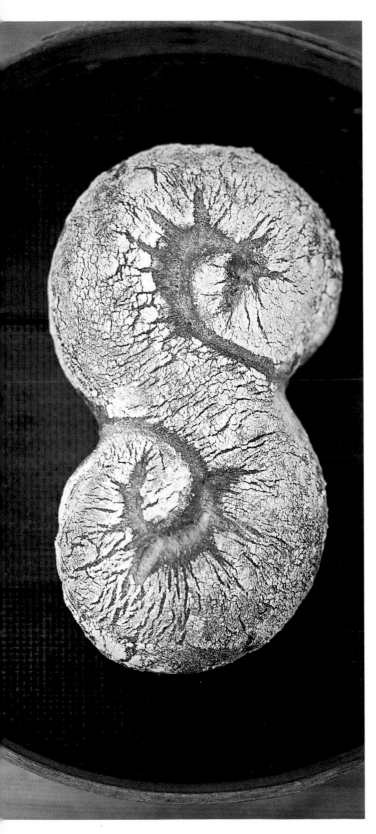

## VARIATION: **Scroll**

SHAPING AND BAKING: **Medium**

YIELD: **4 scrolls**

THE SCROLL IS an attractive bread with a graceful shape, and easier to make than either the baguette or épi. Try using cornmeal on top instead of flour. It is also the best baguette dough for freezing for later use.

**Prepare Formula One (Baguette Dough) through the last stage of step 6, Preshaping/Shaping** (see pages 58–62), rolling out the dough longer and thinner to 20 inches (50 cm) instead of the 14-inch (35-cm) baguette size.

### 7. Final Proof/Panning

Take the 20-inch (50 cm) rolled-out dough and loosely coil up the ends in opposite directions to create an "S" shape.

Place the scrolls on a flour- or cornmeal-dusted couche. (Ground cornmeal provides a nice warm colour and texture to the finished bread.) Cover with a sheet of plastic and let rest for at least 50 minutes.

Gently transfer to a lightly flour-dusted peel or the back of a parchment-lined sheet pan.

7a. Rolling the dough to create the scroll shape

7b. The scrolls rest on a cornmeal-dusted couche.

8. The scrolls are ready to bake. Notice the relaxed shape to the overproofed dough.

### 8. Scoring

The scroll bread is not scored. To prevent the bread from tearing during the bake, the dough should be almost over-proofed before being put in the oven. To test if the bread is ready, push on the dough with your finger. It should show a slight indentation and should have almost no spring back. If the dough collapses upon compression, the proofing has gone too far.

**Follow the remaining steps in the Baguette main formula:**

Just prior to putting the scrolls in the oven, take a water-soaked towel and place it in the steamer pan. Make sure that the towel is completely contained in the pan.

Transfer the scrolls into the oven, using either the peel or sheet-pan method.

When the scrolls attain a golden colour, occasionally open the oven door to allow excess steam to escape. Continue baking for a minimum of 30 minutes, propping the oven door open at the top, using a wooden spoon, for the last 2 minutes.

When the scrolls are done baking, remove them from the oven and place on a wire rack to cool.

## Your SIGNATURE SHAPE

Though the baguette has a very specific, traditional shape, the dough itself is extremely versatile and can be manipulated in a number of ways. Perhaps you want a spiral-shaped bread instead of a scroll, or sandwich rolls for lunch. Or, be adventurous and try a braid! Whatever your fancy, experimenting with shaping and scoring allows you to create your own signature bread form.

# VARIATION: **Breadsticks**

SHAPING AND BAKING: **Easy**

YIELD: **About 20 breadsticks**

THIS IS A GREAT VARIATION to make if you have some dough left over from a batch of baguettes. Experiment with combinations of cheeses, flavoured oils, herbs, and spices and develop your own signature breadsticks. Breadsticks pair well with wine and cheese, are a nice complement to homemade soup, and make lovely gifts, too.

**Prepare Formula One (Baguette Dough) through step 4, Stretch and Fold/Degassing.** (See pages 58–60).

> **ADDITIONAL SPECIAL EQUIPMENT**
> Pastry wheel
> Rolling pin

## 5. Dividing

Invert the container onto a lightly floured table and let gravity release the dough naturally from the container. Do not divide the dough.

## 6. Preshaping/Shaping

With a rolling pin, roll out dough to ⅜ inch (1 cm) thick on a lightly floured surface.

Brush the top with plain or flavoured olive oil and sprinkle with toppings (grated cheese, herbs, spices, seeds) if desired. To achieve an even flavour distribution, you can premix the seeds, herbs, and spices together before sprinkling them on the dough.

Fold one-third of the dough into the centre, then fold the remaining one-third on top. Folding the dough creates the separate layers in the breadsticks. Cover with a sheet of plastic and allow to rest for 20 minutes.

## 7. Final Proof/Panning

Roll out the dough again to ⅜ inch (1 cm) thick on a lightly floured surface.

Using a pastry wheel, cut into even strips about ½ inch (1 cm) thick. A ruler or the edge of a rolling pin helps to guide the pastry wheel and keep the strips straight.

With each hand on an end of the breadstick, twist the breadsticks by rolling one hand forward and one hand backward. For an alternative shape, take twisted dough lengths and coil up into round disks. Straight sticks are quicker to make and bake, but coiling the strips into disks is a simple way to add variety.

Place on a parchment-lined sheet pan and let rest for 30 minutes.

## 8. Scoring

No scoring is necessary since the breadsticks are cut completely down the sides.

## 9. Baking

Just before baking, brush the tops of the breadsticks or disks with some olive oil. For extra-crunchy breadsticks, skip the oil on top. Bake at 450°F (230°C, gas mark 8) for 10 to 12 minutes (12 to 15 minutes for the disks).

## 10. Cooling/Storage

Cool the breadsticks completely on a wire rack and enjoy immediately or store in an airtight container for up to 5 days.

6a. Sprinkle the dough with desired toppings to add flavour.

6b. The dough is folded into thirds.

7a. Cut the breadsticks into even strips.

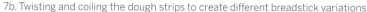

7b. Twisting and coiling the dough strips to create different breadstick variations

DOUGH PREPARATION: **Easy**

SHAPING AND BAKING: **Medium**

YIELD: **4 medium loaves or 8 to 16 smaller breads**

TOTAL TIME: **Approximately 4 hours and 10 minutes over 2 days**

# FORMULA TWO: Ciabatta Dough

THE CIABATTA IS a wonderfully casual Italian bread that has become a staple in bakeries everywhere. The first time this formula is mixed into a slack mass of dough, you may wonder whether you have made a mistake. Do not despair! The dough is wet by design: The high water content in combination with the poolish enables the ciabatta to build its famously airy pockets and delicious flavour. While at first the wetness of the dough may be a challenge to handle, the ciabatta's simplicity, flavour, and versatility will encourage you to persevere!

## POOLISH

| Ingredient | Metric | Weight | Volume | Baker's % |
|---|---|---|---|---|
| Bread flour | 330 g | 11.6 oz | | 100 |
| Water, 70°F (21°C) | 330 g | 11.6 oz | 355 ml | 100 |
| Instant yeast | Pinch | Pinch | Pinch | 1 |

Mix the poolish the day before baking. Combine the bread flour, water, and instant yeast in a bowl and mix by hand with a spoon until smooth. The poolish will have a very wet consistency. Cover it with a plastic lid or plastic wrap so that no crust can form on the poolish and allow it to ferment overnight for about 16 hours at room temperature (68°F to 70°F [20°C to 21°C]).

## FINAL DOUGH

| Ingredient | Metric | Weight | Volume | Baker's % |
|---|---|---|---|---|
| Bread flour | 613 g | 1 lb + 5.6 oz | | 100 |
| Water, 102°F (39°C) | 405 g | 14.3 oz | 415 ml | 66 |
| Instant yeast | 2.6 g | 0.09 oz | ¾ tsp | 1 |
| Salt | 18 g | 0.6 oz | 3½ tsp | 3 |
| Poolish | All of it | All of it | All of it | 107 |

3. Pour the dough into an oiled proofing container.

## STRETCH AND FOLD with Ciabatta

The ciabatta dough is very wet and sticky, making it tricky to handle, especially in the early stages of the stretch and folds. To help prevent the dough from sticking to your hands, fill a bowl with water and dip your hands into it before handling the dough. Doing this will make the stretch and folds much more manageable.

### 1. Mise en Place

Prepare all equipment and scale all ingredients.

**ADDITIONAL SPECIAL EQUIPMENT**
Proofing container
Dough divider
Couche
Proofing board
Peel or sheet pan
Baking stone
Steaming tray

### 2. Mixing

Using a 5-quart (5 L) stand mixer with a dough hook attachment, place the bread flour, water, instant yeast, salt, and poolish in the mixer and mix on low speed for a total of 6 minutes, stopping the mixer every 2 minutes to scrape down any dry matter sticking to the sides and bottom of the bowl.

After all the ingredients have been incorporated, increase the mixing speed to medium and mix for an additional minute or so. Due to the high hydration, or water content, of this dough, it is almost impossible to perform a gluten window test. Rely on the timer (and the senses) to determine when the mixing is done.

### 3. Fermentation

Coat a proofing container with nonstick cooking spray and pour the dough into it. Check the temperature of the dough with a thermometer probe—it should be between 75°F and 78°F (24°C to 26°C).

### 4. Stretch and Folds/Degassing

After pouring the dough into the proofing container, let it rest for 30 minutes and then give it one stretch-and-fold sequence (see chapter 2, page 32).

Let the dough rest for another 30 minutes, then give it another stretch and fold.

Repeat the stretch-and-fold process until you have completed a total of 3 or 4 stretch and folds with the dough. You will notice that as the gluten structure builds up with each progressive stretch and fold, the dough becomes stronger and easier to handle.

Finish with another 30-minute rest period.

Preheat the oven with a baking stone and steaming tray in place to 480°F (250°C, gas mark 10) at least an hour before baking.

### 5. Dividing

Generously flour the work surface and invert the container so that the dough releases and falls onto it. Gently coax the dough into a rectangular form, taking care not to expel too many of the gaseous bubbles that will create the airy pockets in the final product.

Ciabatta dough naturally wants to assume a relaxed log shape, but the length can vary depending on the size of your oven and the desired size of the finished loaves. Using a dough divider, divide the dough into even pieces; 4 units will yield medium-size loaves, whereas 16 units will make smaller individual sandwich rolls.

### 6. Preshaping/Shaping

After dividing the dough into units, gently place them on a heavily floured couche. Some bakers may want to divide this dough by weight instead of visually—any small dough pieces added during dividing to achieve the desired weight should now be on top of the dough pieces.

To help the ciabatta keep its shape, it is good to form pleated ridges with the couche between the loaves (see page 63 of the Baguette formula, and page 58, for a more detailed description of making the pleated ridges).

5. Dividing the ciabatta dough, using a dough divider

### 7. Final Proof/Panning

Cover the loaves with a flour-dusted couche and let proof for 30 to 45 minutes. If the dough seems a bit slack and does not want to retain its shape, the proofing time can be closer to 30 minutes.

### 8. Scoring

No scoring is necessary with this dough, due to its relaxed nature.

## MORE DOUGH Than the Oven Can Handle?

You will get the best results from baking if all loaves receive equal treatment, and that includes baking them all at the same time. But size constraints of ovens, coupled with other factors, sometimes make this ideal scenario impossible. If all the bread cannot fit in the oven in one bake, place the loaves that will be baked second in the refrigerator. This process is known as *retarding* the dough: It slows down the fermentation cycle and is meant to compensate for the extra time the dough will be proofing.

Ideally, retarding begins about three-quarters of the way into the final proofing cycle (or 20 to 30 minutes for this ciabatta formula). What if you only just realise they won't all fit just when it is time to bake? Simply refrigerate as soon as you recognise the dilemma.

6. A variety of ciabatta loaves on a flour-dusted couche

## 9. Baking

Prepare a water-soaked facecloth for the steaming tray and set near the oven.

If using a peel to transfer the loaves into the oven, generously sprinkle the peel with cornmeal to prevent the loaves from sticking.

Transfer each loaf onto the peel by lifting the pleat of the couche and rolling the loaf onto the peel, much like a baguette, or place the loaf on the back of a baking sheet lined with parchment paper. In either case, the side of the loaf that was proofing down on the flour should now be the top of the loaf when baking in the oven.

After loading the loaves into the oven, place the water-soaked facecloth in the steaming tray. Be sure that you have your hands and arms protected and remove them quickly from the oven to avoid any unpleasant encounters with the steam.

Bake for 35 to 40 minutes at 480°F (250°C, gas mark 9). The loaves should have a blistery golden crust. If you notice the loaf getting too dark after 25 minutes, cover with aluminum foil and reduce the temperature of the oven by 30°F to 40°F (-1°C to 4°C). Two minutes before the end of the baking cycle, prop the oven door open with a wooden spoon to allow any extra steam to escape.

## 10. Cooling/Storage

Remove the ciabatta loaves from the oven and cool completely on a wire rack.

Breads made purely with bread flour (white flour), such as the ciabatta, do not offer as long a shelf life as those made with whole grain. Therefore, it is best to enjoy the ciabatta within a few days of baking. Otherwise, wrap tightly in plastic and freeze for up to 4 weeks.

## TRANSFERRING
## Ciabatta or Long Twists

An easy way to move longer pieces of dough, such as ciabatta or twists, is to mimic playing the accordion: Take each end in one hand and simultaneously lift and scoop the dough together, letting it compress slightly. Let the centre of the dough touch the peel first and pull the ends out to its original length when laying them on the peel.

## VARIATION: **Twist Sticks**

SHAPING AND BAKING: **Easy**

YIELD: **4 to 6 long sticks**

THIS VARIATION is literally a quick twist on the ciabatta loaf and, with the addition of sesame or poppy seeds, it has a mildly nutty flavour. The twisted dough not only produces a rustic decorative pattern across the bread, but its structure lends itself nicely to what I refer to as the casual "twist-and-take" technique of sharing bread at a meal.

**Prepare Formula Two (Ciabatta Dough) through step 5, dividing the dough into 4 to 6 long pieces.** (See pages 70–73.)

### 6. Preshaping/Shaping

Line the couche with flour, sesame seeds, or poppy seeds (or any combination thereof).

Lay the long dough pieces onto the bed of flour/seeds and support the sides of the dough with the pleated ridges of the couche between the loaves.

**Follow the remaining steps of the Ciabatta formula:**

Cover the loaves with a flour-dusted couche and let proof for 30 to 45 minutes.

Prepare a water-soaked facecloth for the steaming tray and set near the oven.

If using a peel to transfer the loaves into the oven, sprinkle the peel with cornmeal to prevent them from sticking.

Just before baking, twist the proofed dough 5 or 6 times in the same direction over the entire length of the loaf, to create the twist effect. I find it easiest to twist one end 2 or 3 times clockwise, then move to the other end and twist two or three times counterclockwise (to get the twist to go in the same direction). Place the dough on a peel or the back of a parchment-lined sheet pan.

After loading the loaves into the oven, place the water-soaked facecloth in the steaming tray. Be sure that you have your hands and arms protected, and remove them quickly from the oven to avoid any unpleasant encounters with the steam.

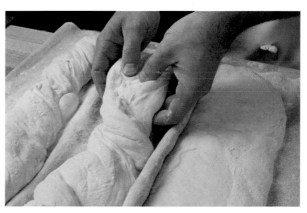

6. The proofed dough is twisted into shape.

Bake for approximately 25 to 30 minutes. The loaves should have a blistery golden crust. Two minutes before the end of the baking cycle, prop the oven door open with a wooden spoon to allow any extra steam to escape.

Remove the twist loaves from the oven and cool completely on a wire rack.

## VARIATION: **Focaccia**

SHAPING AND BAKING: **Easy**

YIELD: **1 sheet pan (13 × 18 inches [33 × 46 cm]) of focaccia**

BAKING FOCACCIA is one of the quickest and easiest ways to make friends. There is no sophisticated shaping involved, no transferring from the peel into the oven, and the combinations of toppings and flavours are endless. It's the perfect item to bring along to a potluck dinner or picnic. Whatever the occasion, you simply cannot go wrong with focaccia.

**Prepare Formula Two (Ciabatta Dough) through step 4, Stretch and Folds/Degassing.** (See pages 70–72.)

> **ADDITIONAL SPECIAL EQUIPMENT**
> Half sheet pan (13" × 10" [33 × 25.4 cm])
> Focaccia toppings

### 5. Dividing

No dividing is necessary for focaccia.

### 6. Preshaping/Shaping

Preheat the oven to 450°F (230°C, gas mark 8). The baking stone and steaming tray are not necessary.

Prepare a half sheet pan by brushing or spraying the bottom and sides with olive oil.

Place the entire dough on the sheet pan. Add some olive oil to the top of the dough to prevent your fingers from sticking. Spread your fingers apart like a pianist and, using your fingertips, gently compress the dough outward toward the edges of the pan. Don't worry if the dough does not reach the edges at first—the dough will eventually relax, and further compressions during the final proofing stage will allow the dough to spread.

6. Use your fingertips to dimple the dough to the outer edges of the sheet pan.

### 7. Final Proof/Panning

Let the dough rest for 10 minutes, then give it another set of compressions across the top. This creates a dimpling effect on the surface. Continue this process for a total of 30 minutes, compressing the dough every 10 minutes with your fingertips, gently coaxing the dough out farther toward the edges each time.

After the second compression, add any desired toppings to the focaccia, with the exception of cheese—this is added later during the baking to avoid burning. If you prefer your focaccia unadorned, simply brush the top with some plain or flavoured olive oil and sprinkle with herbs and sea salt if desired.

After the last compression, let the dough rest for another 15 minutes.

### 8. Scoring

No scoring is necessary.

### 9. Baking

Place the sheet pan in the oven and bake for approximately 30 minutes.

If you want to add cheese to the focaccia, do so after it has been baking for about 20 minutes.

### 10. Cooling/Storage

Remove the focaccia from the oven and let cool in the sheet pan on a wire rack for at least 30 minutes.

Cut when ready to serve and serve warm (not hot) or at room temperature.

Focaccia can be covered with plastic wrap and kept overnight to reheat the next day, but it's never as good as the day it is baked!

7. With the exception of cheese, add the toppings to the focaccia after the second compression.

9. If desired, sprinkle with cheese after 20 minutes of baking.

DOUGH PREPARATION: **Easy**

SHAPING AND BAKING: **Easy**

YIELD: **2 loaves**

TOTAL TIME: **Approximately 5 hours over 2 days**

# FORMULA THREE: Whole Wheat Dough

**WHOLE-GRAIN BREADS** become more popular as people grow more aware of the grains' health benefits. When sliced, this bread reveals a fairly dense crumb structure with the hearty texture of the evenly dispersed seeds. The added fiber and protein makes it the perfect companion for breakfast, and the nutty flavour of the seeds becomes even richer with toasting. Children will relish lunches packed with sandwiches made with this bread, and tree nut–related allergies are not a concern because it is made from seeds.

## BIGA

| Ingredient | Metric | Weight | Volume | Baker's % |
|---|---|---|---|---|
| Bread flour | 180 g | 6.3 oz | | 100 |
| Water, 70°F (21°C) | 107 g | 3.8 oz | 120 ml | 60 |
| Instant yeast | 1.3 g | 0.05 oz | 1¼ tsp | 0.7 |

Place the bread flour, water, and instant yeast in the bowl of a stand mixer and mix with a dough hook attachment for about 3 minutes. The biga will feel tight and rubbery after it has been mixed; do not add any additional water. Place the biga in a proofing container coated with nonstick cooking spray, cover with a lid or plastic wrap, and allow to sit out at room temperature for 1 to 2 hours. It should double in size. The biga is now ready to use, but its flavour will improve if refrigerated overnight and used the next day. To hold the biga overnight, gently degas by pressing down on it with your hands, cover it, and place it in the refrigerator overnight.

## FINAL DOUGH

| Ingredient | Metric | Weight | Volume | Baker's % |
|---|---|---|---|---|
| Whole wheat flour | 657 g | 1 pound, 7.1 oz | | 100 |
| Water, 95°F* (35°C) | 462 g | 1 pound, 0.3 oz | 475 ml | 70 |
| Honey | 52 g | 1.85 oz | 55 ml | 8 |
| Instant yeast | 2.5 g | 0.1 oz | ¾ tsp | 0.4 |
| Salt | 16 g | 0.58 oz | 3 tsp | 2.5 |
| Biga | All of it | All of it | All of it | 40 |
| Sunflower seeds, roasted** | 50 g | 1.75 oz | | 7 |
| Pumpkin seeds, roasted** | 50 g | 1.75 oz | | 7 |
| Sesame seeds, roasted** | 50 g | 1.75 oz | | 7 |

*If the biga has not been refrigerated, use 75°F (24°C) water instead.

**The use of seeds is optional.

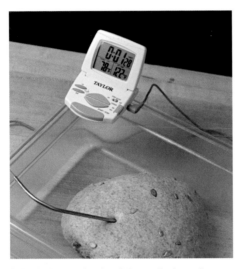

2. With the dough mixing on low speed, add the seeds.

3. After placing the dough in an oiled proofing container, check its temperature.

6. Shape the loaves, roll in oats if desired, and place into pan.

### 1. Mise en Place

Gather all equipment and prescale all ingredients

**ADDITIONAL SPECIAL EQUIPMENT**
   9 x 5-inch (23 x 13 cm) baking loaf pans
   Steaming tray

### 2. Mixing

Place the whole wheat flour, water, honey, instant yeast, salt, and biga into a 5-quart (5 L) stand mixer bowl. Using a dough hook attachment, mix the ingredients on low speed for approximately 4 minutes. Increase mixing speed to medium and mix for an additional 2 minutes.

Add the optional sunflower, pumpkin, and sesame seeds on low speed until fully incorporated. *Note: If you are planning to make the pita version, do not add seeds; or add seeds to only half of the dough being baked.*

### 3. Fermentation

Place the dough in a proofing container coated with non-stick cooking spray and check the temperature with a digital thermometer probe; the ideal temperature is 75°F to 78°F (24°C to 26°C). Cover with plastic wrap or lid and allow to rest for 45 minutes.

### 4. Stretch and Folds/Degassing

After the dough has rested for 45 minutes, give the dough one stretch and fold and let rest again for 45 minutes.

Preheat the oven with a baking stone and steaming tray in place to 450°F (230°C, gas mark 8) at least an hour before baking.

### 5. Dividing

Divide dough in half (approximately two 730-gram [26 ounce] pieces).

### 6. Preshaping/Shaping

On a lightly floured surface, shape into a squat oval loaf (see Shaping Basics, page 46) and place immediately into a baking loaf pan coated with nonstick cooking spray.

### 7. Final Proof/Panning

Cover the loaves with a sheet of plastic and let them proof for 1 to 1½ hours at room temperature. To check if they are done proofing, press gently into the dough with your fingers; the dough should recover slowly to almost the original size, but a slight indentation will be present.

### 8. Scoring

There is no need to score these loaves.

### 9. Baking

Prepare a water-soaked facecloth for the steaming tray.

Place the loaves in the oven.

Lay the wet facecloth completely in the tray to create a burst of steam. As always, make sure your hands, arms, and face are well protected from the heat and steam.

Bake for 20 minutes at 450°F (230°C, gas mark 8). Keeping the loaves in the oven, adjust the oven temperature to 380°F (190°C, gas mark 5) and bake for an additional 20 to 30 minutes. The loaves will be in the oven for a total of 40 to 50 minutes. Cover with aluminum foil if the loaves get too dark too quickly.

Remove the loaves from the pan and place back in the oven directly on the wire rack for an additional 5 minutes. This ensures even browning on the sides and gives the loaf a bit more strength.

### 10. Cooling/Storage

Remove the loaves from the oven and set on a wire cooling rack.

Thanks to the moisture-holding capacities of the whole wheat, this bread has a longer shelf life than a loaf of bread made with refined bread flour. You can easily keep this loaf in a paper bag for 3 to 4 days, depending on the environment. It also freezes well—just wrap tightly in plastic and freeze for up to 2 months.

7. Upon gentle compression, the proofed dough recovers slowly back to almost, but not quite, its original shape.

## REMOVING LOAVES from Pans

Sometimes, despite our best efforts, the loaves do not release as effortlessly from the pans as we hope for. If this happens, it may help to invert the pan and gently bang the edge downward onto the edge of the countertop. Make sure to hit only the pan edge with the countertop edge, not the bread itself. A few taps are usually all it takes to help ease the loaf out, but if you find yourself relentlessly banging away, then it's time to enlist the aid of a trusty knife.

## Quick OAT COVERING

Try an easy decorative effect for either the whole wheat loaves or rolls (see page 82): Moisten the top of the shaped dough by either rolling it over a wet facecloth or misting with a water spray bottle and then roll the moistened side in whole rolled oats or oat bran. Once the oats have been applied, place either the loaf into the pan or the roll onto the parchment-lined sheet pan for the final proof.

## VARIATION: **Round Rolls**

SHAPING AND BAKING:  **Easy**

YIELD:  **14 rolls or 7 rolls and 1 loaf**

**Prepare Formula Three (Whole Wheat Dough) through step 4, Stretch and Folds/Degassing.**
(See pages 78–80.)

> **ADDITIONAL SPECIAL EQUIPMENT**
> Sheet pan
> Parchment paper

### 5. Dividing

Using a scale and a dough divider, divide dough into 16 equal pieces (90 to 95 grams [3.2 to 3.4 ounce] each).

### 6. Preshaping/Shaping

Using your hands, shape the dough pieces into round balls (see Shaping Basics, page 44–45.) For a decorative effect, see "Quick Oat Covering," page 81.

### 7. Final Proof/Panning

Place the rolls on a parchment-lined sheet pan (6 to 8 per sheet pan, evenly spaced) and cover with a piece of plastic wrap.

Preheat oven with steaming tray to 450°F (230°C, gas mark 8).

Allow to proof at room temperature for about 1 hour.

**Follow the remaining steps in the Whole wheat Dough formula:**

Prepare a water-soaked facecloth for the steaming tray and set aside.

Place the rolls in the oven and then lay the cloth completely in the tray to create a burst of steam.

Bake on a parchment-lined sheet pan at 450°F (230°C, gas mark 8), with steam, for a total of 18 to 22 minutes.

Remove the rolls from the oven and set on a wire cooling rack.

6. Shape the dough into round balls.

7. Whole wheat rolls baking in the oven

## VARIATION: **Savoury Pizzalets**

SHAPING AND BAKING: **Easy**

YIELD: **14 pizzalets or**
**7 pizzalets and 1 loaf**

WITH THEIR ENDLESS VARIETY of toppings, these small pizzas are great as an appetizer, a quick portable lunch, or even as a dinner paired with soup or salad. Everyone's preferences can be accommodated; a little Boursin cheese with roasted red pepper or even a quick store-bought pesto sauce can completely change the look and flavour.

**Prepare the Roll Variation of Formula Three (Whole Wheat Dough) through step 6, Preshaping/Shaping.** (See page 82.)

**ADDITIONAL SPECIAL EQUIPMENT**
Savoury toppings

### 7. Final Proof/Panning

Place rolls on a parchment-lined sheet pan, cover with plastic wrap, and allow to proof at room temperature for about 45 minutes.

After 45 minutes, brush the tops of the rolls with plain or savory olive oil.

Using your hands, gently compress the rolls down flat and the sides out so that a small dish cavity forms in the centre. If the dough feels tight and wants to shrink back in, let it rest for 15 minutes and then compress down and out once more with your hands. The disks should be around 4 inches (10 cm) in diameter.

Fill the centre with a topping of your choice. It can be as simple as a bit of tomato sauce and cheese or some roasted garlic, or you can let your imagination run wild. For specific ideas, refer to the savoury filling formulas on pages 157–159).

### 8. SCORING

There is no need to score this variation.

7a. Gently compress the rolls to create a small cavity in the centre.

7b. Spoon the topping into the centre of the pizzalet.

### 9. Baking

Place sheet pan in oven and bake for 15 to 18 minutes at 450°F (230°C, gas mark 8).

### 10. Cooling/Storing

After baking, brush the outer edge of the pizzalet with a savoury olive oil for added flavour and shine.

Enjoy the pizzalets while they are slightly warm or at room temperature. They can be stored overnight in an airtight container and reheated in a toaster oven or conventional oven the next day.

## VARIATION: **Pita Bread**

SHAPING AND BAKING: **Easy**

YIELD: **12 pitas or 6 pitas and 1 loaf**

THIS VERSION OF A PITA is always fun to make because of the dramatic puffing of the dough as it bakes. It is a great way to enlist help in the kitchen, especially if you have young ones around (but anyone young at heart will do!)

**Prepare Roll Variation of Formula Three (Whole Wheat Dough) through step 6** (see page 82), dividing the dough into 12 pieces (130 grams [4.6 ounces] each); do not add the seeds to the formula. Preheat the oven to 500°F (250°C, gas mark 10) with baking stone in place.

> **ADDITIONAL SPECIAL EQUIPMENT**
> Rolling pin

### 7. Final Proof/Panning

After shaping into round rolls, place the dough rolls onto a floured proofing board or table, cover with plastic wrap, and let rest for 15 to 20 minutes.

Using a rolling pin, roll out each ball on a floured surface to a 6-inch (15 cm) -diameter circle.

Cover with plastic wrap and let rest for another 5 minutes.

Roll out the circle of dough again, increasing the size to about 8 to 10 inches (20 to 25 cm) in diameter (approximately ⅛ inch [3 mm] thick).

### 8. Scoring

There is no need to score this variation.

### 9. Baking

Place disks of dough directly on the baking stone in the 500°F (260°C) oven. Do not steam.

Bake for 2 to 4 minutes. The dough should puff up completely like a pillow during the baking process.

### 10. Cooling/Storage

Remove the pitas from the oven and let cool on a wire rack for about 1 minute.

Gently compress downward on the pitas just enough to remove any excess air, but do not flatten them too aggressively or the pocket created may start to stick together.

To store, stack the pitas on top of each other while still warm. Once cool, store in a plastic bag for 1 to 2 days.

7. Roll out the pitas with a rolling pin.

## PITA CHIPS

Pitas can always be made into pita chips. Simply tear the pita into bite-size pieces and place on a sheet pan sprayed with olive oil. Spray the tops of the chips with oil as well and sprinkle with salt and herbs if desired. Place into a 350°F (180°C, gas mark 4) oven and bake until crisp, checking them every 5 minutes or so. Total baking time will be around 10 minutes. Remove from oven, let cool, and store in an airtight container for up to 1 week.

# FORMULA FOUR: **Pane Francese**

PANE FRANCESE HAILS from northern Italy, and its name directly translates to "French bread." As the name implies, this bread has a history connected to both the Romans and the French. Its substantial and hearty golden crust, combined with the open, moist crumb structure, is very much in the style of a French country bread. The size and shapes of these small breads and their very easy formula make them highly recommended for the beginner.

## BIGA

| Ingredient | Metric | Weight | Volume | Baker's % |
|---|---|---|---|---|
| Bread flour | 280 g | 9.8 oz | | 100 |
| Water, 77°F (25°C) | 168 g | 5.9 oz | 180 ml | 60 |
| Instant yeast | 2.1 g | 0.07 oz | 2 tsp | 0.75 |

The biga can be prepared either the day of or the day before baking, whichever fits into your schedule better. Mix the bread flour, water, and instant yeast together in a stand mixer on a slow speed for approximately 3 minutes until all ingredients are incorporated. The biga should feel smooth and tight and somewhat rubbery after being mixed. Do not add any additional water.

Place the biga in a container coated with cooking spray, large enough to accommodate double the initial size of the biga. Cover with a lid or plastic wrap and let the biga stand at room temperature (approximately 68°F to 70°F [20°C to 21°C]) for 1 to 2 hours until it doubles in size. Theoretically the biga is now ready to use, but the flavour of the bread will be improved if the biga rests in the refrigerator overnight. If the biga will not be used until the next day, gently degas it in the oiled proofing container by pressing down on it with your hands, cover with a lid or plastic, and then refrigerate until the next day.

## FINAL DOUGH

| Ingredient | Metric | Weight | Volume | Baker's % |
|---|---|---|---|---|
| Bread flour | 408 g | 14.3 oz | | 100 |
| Biga | All of it | All of it | All of it | 110 |
| Water, 95°F* (35°C) | 294 g | 10.3 oz | 315 ml | 72 |
| Salt | 12 g | 0.4 oz | 2¼ tsp | 3 |

*Note: If the biga has not been refrigerated, use 75°F (24°C) water instead.

2. Cut the biga into smaller pieces and put into the prescaled water.

3. Pour the dough into the prepared container.

As a variation, proof the dough on a bed of sunflower, poppy, or sesame seeds instead of flour. This is an easy way to add colour and texture to the breads.

## 1. Mise en Place

Prepare and scale all ingredients.

**ADDITIONAL SPECIAL EQUIPMENT**
Baking stone
Couche or proofing board
Peel or parchment-lined sheet pan
Steaming tray

## 2. Mixing

Because the biga is less hydrated and contains a lesser percentage of water than the final dough, it needs to be cut into smaller pieces so it can be evenly incorporated into the dough during mixing. For even better results, place the pieces into the prescaled 95°F (35°C) water.

Using a 5-quart (5 L) stand mixer with a dough hook, combine the bread flour, biga, water, and salt on low speed for approximately 4 minutes.

When the ingredients start to come together into the cleanup stage (see page 31), increase the mixing speed to medium for 5 to 6 minutes. To see if the dough is done mixing, take a piece and do a gluten window test. It should be developed to a second-stage window (see Gluten Window Test, page 31) and then taken off the mixer.

## 3. Fermentation

Gently pour the dough into a container coated with non-stick cooking spray. The container should be large enough for the dough mass to double in size.

Cover with a plastic lid and allow the dough to rest for 90 minutes. Plastic wrap may be used as well, as long as it does not come into contact with the surface of the dough.

Preheat the oven to 480°F (250°C, gas mark 10) with a baking stone and steaming tray in place with an hour to go.

## 4. Stretch and Folds/Degassing

Because this formula has a longer mixing time to create strength, this dough does not need a stretch and fold.

### 5. Dividing

Invert the container onto a lightly flour-dusted table.Let gravity do the work—do not bang or scrape out the dough.

Using a dough divider, divide the dough into 16 to 20 small squares, approximately 2 x 2 inches (5 x 5 cm) in size. While care should be taken to keep the sizes uniform, these pieces should be clean cut and in one singular piece; therefore, they do not have to be divided by weight.

### 6. Preshaping/Shaping

This shape requires no additional manipulation. The divided shapes become the shape of the bread.

### 7. Final Proof

Place the pillow-shaped pieces of dough onto a heavily floured couche or proofing board. Whichever side was down after dividing the dough on the table should now be up.

Cover the dough with a cloth and let rest for approximately 45 minutes.

### 8. Scoring

It is not necessary to score this bread, but a single cut down the centre may be made if desired.

### 9. Baking

Prepare a water-soaked facecloth to place in steaming pan, or have the water spray bottle ready.

Transfer the proofed pieces into the oven using either the peel or sheet-pan method (see page 41).

Place the facecloth in the steamer pan, taking care that it is completely contained within the pan. Be sure that your hands and arms are well protected from the resulting quick burst of steam. Alternatively, pour ¼ cup (60 ml) of water directly into the steaming tray to create steam.

Bake for 15 to 18 minutes, until the crust forms a nice golden colour. Prop the oven door open with a wooden spoon handle for the last 2 or 3 minutes of the bake, to allow any extra moisture in the oven to escape.

7. Proof the pane francese on a heavily floured couche or proofing board.

8. If desired, make one single cut down the centre.

### 10. Cooling/Storing

Place the finished bread on a wire rack and allow to cool completely, at least 1 hour.

Pane francese is best enjoyed the day of baking or by the next day at the latest. Otherwise, wrap tightly with plastic wrap and store in the freezer for up to 2 weeks.

## VARIATION: **Fougasse**

SHAPING AND BAKING: **Easy**

YIELD: **3 fougasse**

FOUGASSE IS AN ELEGANT, flat, decorative bread. Its name is derived from the Latin word *focus*, meaning "hearth"; originally it was baked in the ashes of fireplaces.

**Prepare Formula Four (Pane Francese) through step 4.** (See page 86–88.)

> **ADDITIONAL SPECIAL EQUIPMENT**
> Rolling pin
> Pastry brush

### 5. Dividing

Invert the container of dough onto a lightly flour-dusted table. Using a scale and a dough divider, divide into 3 pieces (400-gram [14-ounce] portions) of dough.

### 6. Preshaping/Shaping

Using a rolling pin, roll out the dough to approximately 7 x 9 inches (18 x 23 cm).

Take a dough divider or sharp knife and make five cuts completely through the dough.

Place the fougasse onto a parchment-lined sheet pan. The fougasse will naturally open. Use your hands to gently reshape and extend the dough into the fougasse form.

### 7. Final Proof

Cover the dough with a sheet of plastic or flour-dusted cloth and let rest for about 45 minutes.

### 8. Scoring

The fougasse has already been scored.

6. Making a fougasse is as easy as rolling out the dough, making the cuts, and stretching the fougasse into shape.

## CUTTING Fougasse

The five-cut is a classic fougasse cut, but you are not limited to this shape. Try different shapes and cuts, such as angled parallel cuts extended lengthwise for a longer fougasse, or start with a triangular dough shape instead. With a little experience, you will learn to balance the number of cuts within the size of the dough.

### 9. Baking

Just before baking, brush the top of the fougasse with olive oil. If desired, sprinkle with salt and herbs, such as rosemary, marjoram, and ground sage.

Bake for 15 to 20 minutes. There is no need to add steam into the oven, since the fougasse has been brushed with olive oil.

### 10. Cooling/Storage

After baking, remove the fougasse from the sheet pan and allow to cool on a wire rack.

Due to their relatively thin and delicate shape, fougasse breads are to be enjoyed the day they are baked. It is difficult to freeze them successfully, although it may be possible if you have a vacuum food storage system.

## VARIATION: Stamped Rolls

SHAPING AND BAKING: **Easy**

YIELD: **16 to 20 rolls**

**Prepare Formula Four (Pane Francese) through step 5.** (See pages 86–87.)

> **ADDITIONAL SPECIAL EQUIPMENT**
> Roll stamp (available at specialty stores and online)

6. Press roll stamp into dough after dividing.

### 6. Preshaping/Shaping

Using a spiral or star roll stamp, press the stamp into dough to create the imprinted design, being careful not to cut all the way through the dough.

**Follow the remaining steps for the pane francese:**

Preheat the oven to 480°F (250°C, gas mark 10) with a baking stone and steaming tray in place, for 1 hour.

Place the rolls of dough onto a heavily floured couche or proofing board.

Cover the dough with a cloth and let rest for approximately 45 minutes.

Prepare a water-soaked facecloth to place in steaming pan, or have the water spray bottle ready.

Transfer the proofed pieces into the oven using either the peel or the sheet pan method (see page 41.)

Place the facecloth in the steamer pan. Bake for approximately 20 minutes, until the crust forms a nice golden colour. Prop the oven door open with a wooden spoon handle for the last 2 or 3 minutes of the bake to allow any extra moisture in the oven to escape. Place the finished bread on a wire rack and allow to cool completely, at least 1 hour.

| | |
|---|---|
| DOUGH PREPARATION: | **Easy** |
| SHAPING AND BAKING: | **Easy** |
| YIELD: | **Makes six 10-inch (25 cm) pizzas** |
| TOTAL TIME: | **Approximately 7 to 20 hours over 2 or 3 days (50 minutes of active work)** |

# FORMULA FIVE: Pizza Dough

AT OUR HOUSE, we have a wood-fired oven just beyond our back door. Building it was a labor of love and included the talents of many friends, family, and neighbors who endured long days and late nights of hard work. Now one of our favourite things to do is to make pizzas! Nothing brings people together more quickly than a fun, potluck pizza party, and you certainly do not need a wood-fired oven to yield great pizza. You provide the dough and the oven and your guests bring along the toppings. Anything and everything goes! From classic tomato and mozzarella to more exotic combinations of roasted fennel and walnuts drizzled with a balsamic vinegar, you will be amazed at how creative people will become when it is their turn to top.

## POOLISH

| Ingredient | Metric | Weight | Volume | Baker's % |
|---|---|---|---|---|
| Bread flour | 220 g | 7.75 oz | | 100 |
| Water, 70°F (21°C) | 220 g | 7.75 oz | 240 ml | 100 |
| Instant yeast | 0.25 g | Pinch | Pinch | 0.1 |

Prepare the poolish the night before baking. Combine the bread flour, water, and instant yeast and mix with a spoon or spatula until smooth. It will be very sticky. Cover the bowl with plastic wrap and let stand at room temperature overnight, 12 to 16 hours.

## FINAL DOUGH

| Ingredient | Metric | Weight | Volume | Baker's % |
|---|---|---|---|---|
| Bread flour | 1000 g | 2 lb, 3.25 oz | | 100 |
| Water, 80°F (27°C) | 500 g | 1 lb, 1.6 oz | 535 ml | 50 |
| Instant yeast | 4 g | 0.15 oz | 1¼ tsp | 0.40 |
| Salt | 26 g | 0.90 | 4 tsp | 2.6 |
| Cornmeal | 10 g | 0.35 oz | 2 tsp | 1 |
| Savoury oil mix | 35 g | 1.25 oz | 2 tbsp | 3.5 |
| Poolish | All of it | All of it | All of it | All of it |

To make the savoury oil mix, combine olive oil with your choice of salt, pepper, crushed garlic, and spices. Mix up at least ½ cup (120 ml)—that way you will have some left over to brush on the crust of the pizza.

## Planning for DESSERT?

If dessert pizzas are on the menu, substitute plain olive oil for the savoury oil mix. After mixing, remove half of the dough from the mixing bowl, cover with plastic, and set aside for dessert pizzas. Add dried savoury herbs and spices to the remaining dough in the mixing bowl.

### 1. Mise en Place

Prepare and scale all ingredients for dough and prepare all desired toppings for pizza (see Pizza Toppings, page 96).

> **ADDITIONAL SPECIAL EQUIPMENT**
> Rolling pin
> Peel or parchment-lined sheet pan
> Baking stone
> Pastry brush

### 2. Mixing

Using a 5-quart (5 L) or larger stand mixer with a dough hook attachment, place the bread flour, water, instant yeast, salt, cornmeal, and poolish in the bowl and mix on low speed for approximately 4½ minutes.

After the ingredients have been incorporated, increase the mixing speed to medium and mix for 2 to 3 minutes, slowly adding the savoury oil to the dough. (See tip, above left, if making dessert pizzas.)

### 3. Fermentation

Coat a proofing container with nonstick cooking spray and place the dough in the container. Test the internal temperature of the dough and be sure it is around 75°F (24°C). If it is not, place the container in a warm environment until this temperature is achieved, or plan on extending the proofing time.

3. The pizza dough after mixing and ready for fermentation

### 4. Stretch and Folds/Degassing

With the dough in the proofing container, cover and let it rest for 45 minutes and then give it one stretch-and-fold sequence (see page 32).

Cover and let rest for another 45 minutes.

### 5. Dividing

Turn the dough out onto a floured surface and use a dough divider and a scale to divide the dough into 6 pieces (220 g [7.75-ounce] each).

### 6. Preshaping/Shaping

Preshape the units into rounds (see pages 44–45). Coat the rounds with olive oil or savoury mixture and place 6 rounds on a sheet pan. Cover with plastic wrap and set in the refrigerator to rest.

6. Place the rounds on a sheet pan and cover with plastic wrap.

## 7. Final Proof

The final proofing occurs slowly at a lower temperature in the refrigerator. The optimum proofing time is between 4 and 6 hours, but the timing on this stage for this dough is a bit more flexible than for most others, and you can easily hold this dough until the next day. You can also place the dough rounds carefully into individual quart-size freezer bags and freeze for up to 2 weeks. To use, remove from freezer and let thaw in the refrigerator.

## 8. Scoring

About 90 minutes before baking, preheat the oven to 500°F (250°C, gas mark 10) with the baking stone in place.

Pizzas are not scored, but they are formed into thin disks and covered with a variety of toppings. To form the pizzas, remove the rounds from the refrigerator and let sit at room temperature for about 15 minutes. With floured hands and working on a floured surface, press the ball of dough down so that it flattens.

With a rolling pin, roll the dough out in a circular shape (or oval shape, depending on the width of your peel) to a thickness of approximately ⅜ inch (1 cm) thick, or about 10 inches (25 cm) in diameter.

Lay the pizza on a cornmeal-dusted peel or a parchment-lined sheet pan. Using a pastry brush, brush the outer edge of the pizza with some savoury olive oil, trying to not get it on the peel if you can help it. You can brush the entire pizza if desired, but it is not necessary. Apply the desired sauce and toppings (see Pizza Toppings, page 96.)

8a. With your hands, press the dough ball flat.

8b. Roll the pizza dough out to ⅜ inch (1 cm) thick.

8c. Brush the oil around the outer edge of the pizza.

## ROLLING OUT
### Pizza Dough

When rolling pizza dough, roll it out once, let it rest for a few minutes, then roll it out again to the final shape. Take care that it does not become too thin, or the toppings will stick to the stone!

8d. Add the toppings to the pizza.

## 9. Baking

Transfer the pizza into the oven and onto the baking stone. Pizzas are baked at a higher oven temperature than are most breads, and the bottom of the pizza should quickly bake and seal from the radiant heat of the stone.

Bake each pizza until the desired crust texture is achieved, between 7 and 15 minutes, depending on the oven and personal preference.

## 10. Cooling/Storage

Needless to say, most people like to enjoy their pizza hot and straight from the oven—just be careful not to burn the roof of your mouth! If you are serving a crowd buffet style, it is okay to let the pizza sit out at room temperature for about an hour, but any longer than that and food safety police may come knocking at your door.

Wrap any uneaten portions and refrigerate. You can reheat the pizza the next day or eat it cold if you like, but it is never as good as it is hot from the oven.

## PIZZA TOPPINGS

Pizza toppings are whatever you want them to be, so let your culinary delights run wild! That said, it is best to keep things simple, highlighting just two or three flavours at a time. Try a combination of shredded mozzarella with some harder cheese, such as Asiago, Parmesan, or Gruyère. Sauces can range from traditional tomato to a rich creamy white sauce or a zippy vodka sauce. Steam vegetables ahead so they are tender, and always precook meats before using them as toppings.

Some favourite combinations to try include:

- Heirloom tomatoes, fresh mozzarella, and basil
- Baby shrimp with shaved garlic and fresh corn
- Roasted eggplant and goat cheese
- Gorgonzola with poached pears and walnuts

- Barbecued chicken with caramelized onions
- Spicy Italian sausage, roasted red peppers, and steamed broccoli rabe
- Baby spinach with sliced prosciutto and garlic

- Grilled corn kernels with avocado and fresh cilantro
- Smoked salmon with capers and crème fraîche
- Sliced boiled red potatoes, Gruyère, and bacon

## VARIATION: Dessert Pizza

SHAPING AND BAKING: **Easy**

YIELD: **About six 10-inch (25 cm) pizzas**

PIZZA FOR DESSERT? Are you intrigued? This is not the overly sweet, cookie-dough-with-frosting approach. In fact, it is the same formula for the regular pizza—the only difference is in the toppings: fruit, chocolate, crumbs, and more. The result is a surprising and flavourful end to a meal and pairs perfectly with some ice cream on the side and a cup of rich espresso or coffee.

**Prepare Formula Five (Pizza Dough) up to step 7, Final Proof.** (See pages 92–95.) See Planning for Dessert, page 94, and omit the savory herbs.

### 8. Scoring

Follow the steps to shape the pizzas in the main formula (see pages 94–95).

Instead of savoury toppings, choose ingredients that traditionally are headlines for desserts. One of my favourite combinations is a thin layer of chocolate hazelnut spread (such as Nutella) topped with sliced bananas and a little cinnamon on top. Or sauté some apple slices in melted butter, vanilla bean, and sugar, allow them to cool, then place them on the pizza and sprinkle some crumb topping over before baking. Scan your favourite dessert recipes and see if you can come up with a pizza to match it! (See Dessert, Anyone? at right for more ideas.)

### 9. Baking

These pizzas can be baked like regular pizzas, although some ingredients, such as powdered sugar and whipped cream, should be added after baking. It is also possible to bake a plain dessert pizza dough and add toppings just before serving, such as pastry cream and fresh seasonal berries.

### 10. Cooling and Storage

The dessert pizzas are best enjoyed immediately, but they are also fine cold from the refrigerator the next day. Just cover with some plastic wrap and store overnight.

## DESSERT, ANYONE?

If you have never tried a dessert pizza before, you are missing out on a good thing. Here are a few more mouthwatering suggestions:

- Thinly sliced fresh nectarines drizzled with a vanilla-flavoured simple syrup and topped with whipped cream
- Candied ginger pieces brushed with honey
- Bananas, chocolate sauce, and chopped walnuts, served with vanilla ice cream
- Roasted pineapple slices sprinkled with brown sugar
- Blanched rhubarb sprinkled with sugar and with fresh strawberries and whipped cream.

# VARIATION: **Easy Rolls**

SHAPING AND BAKING:  **Easy**

YIELD:  **4 rolls per pizza unit
(24 rolls for entire formula)**

**SOMETIMES IT IS POSSIBLE** to have too much of a good thing, and pizza can be one of them. This dough makes wonderful and tasty dinner rolls that are a cinch to make. They are almost as popular as the pizza and, whenever these rolls get served, guests always clamor for more. They are a perfect accompaniment to a soup or salad and make a quick sandwich themselves.

**Prepare Formula Five (Pizza Dough) through step 7, Final Proof.** (See pages 92–95.)

### 8. Scoring

The rolls are not scored. Take a round pizza unit (do not flatten the dough down) and make a crossed indentation with a dough divider, thereby dividing the round visually into quarters. The indentations should be substantial but not deep enough to actually cut through the dough.

Brush olive oil over the tops and sprinkle with some toppings if desired, such as coarse salt, Parmesan cheese, crushed garlic, or other herbs or spices. Place on a peel or parchment-lined sheet pan.

### 9. Baking

Bake in a hot oven, around 450°F (230°C, gas mark 8) to 500°F (250°C, gas mark 10), for 10 to 15 minutes. The rolls will turn a nice dark golden brown on the tops.

### 10. Cooling/Storage

These easy rolls are best enjoyed hot from the oven, but let them cool down a bit so at least they can be handled. They are easily divided along the indentations, so guests can help themselves by breaking off the units.

8. Use the dough divider to create a crossed indentation, then brush olive oil over the top.

# Philosophy of Baking:
## THE JOURNEY OF BREAD

Remember a time when you were overwhelmed by the beauty of your surroundings. Perhaps it was during a summer hike amid the mountains, or on a walk on a windswept beach beneath an impossibly blue sky. Maybe it was even in the middle of a bustling city. Wherever it was, your senses were in overdrive, hungry to absorb all the details of the moment. Most likely there was simply too much at once to remember.

If you visited that place a second time, you probably noticed things that you hadn't before. Perhaps it was the wildflower that took root in the crevice of a rock, or the pattern in the canvas of wet sand left by the pipers, or the shadow cast by a building in the afternoon's waning sunlight. And if you revisited these places several times, or incorporated them into your daily life, the details of the surroundings would become ingrained in your memory.

Your experience of the place would be as familiar and comfortable as a well-worn book or a favourite pair of broken-in jeans.

So it is with baking bread: a continuous journey of constant discovery. The first few times you bake bread may be awkward, even intimidating—and that is okay. You can't learn to swim without getting wet, so jump in and get your hands in the dough! One thing is for certain: You will make mistakes. Things will not be perfect. Bread will be burned or underbaked. Shapes may not come out as intended.

As time goes by and your experience increases, you will sense the bigger picture and will grow more in tune with the details. How is the dough feeling? Do you need to hold back a bit on the water? Or add a bit more? Is it proofing faster than the formula indicates? Or does it need to rest a little longer?

Becoming one with the dough takes time, but as you do, your bread baking will become more intuitive. You will make adjustments without agonizing over them. The path you take will become well trodden, each step more familiar and natural. And while there is no such thing as "perfect," practice will get you as close as you can. So embrace the journey and let it begin!

# FORMULA SIX: Bagel Dough

THE ORIGIN OF THE BAGEL is still hotly debated. One version tells the tale of the first bagel being created by a Viennese baker as an homage to King Jan of Poland. Through his exceptional cavalry skills, this king helped defeat the Turks in 1683, and the ring-shaped bagel, representing a round stirrup, was invented to honour him. Some historians dismiss this story as folklore, citing evidence of the *bagel* describing a baked good given as a gift to women in childbirth and midwives in the early 1600s. In any case, we do know bagels were intro-duced to the United States in the late 1800s by German and Polish immigrants.

Homemade bagels are a rare treat, but for those who are brave enough to subject their equipment to the stiff dough and arduous mixing, the rewards will be plenty.

This is an authentic bagel formula with a few hard-to-find ingredients: high-gluten flour and diastatic malt. If you cannot pro-cure them, you can use regular bread flour and omit the malt completely, knowing that the texture and flavour will be a little different (but will still yield a great bagel!).

## FINAL DOUGH

| Ingredient | Metric | Weight | Volume | Baker's % |
|---|---|---|---|---|
| Bread flour | 413 g | 14.5 oz | | 50 |
| High-gluten flour* or bread flour | 413 g | 14.5 oz | | 50 |
| Water, 72°F (22°C) | 491 g | 1 lb, 1.3 oz | 500 ml | 59.4 |
| Instant yeast | 5 g | 0.17 oz | 1½ tsp | 0.6 |
| Salt | 16 g | 0.56 oz | 2½ tsp | 1.9 |
| Diastatic malt* (optional) | 12 g | 0.42 oz | 4 tsp | 1.4 |

*Available through specialty stores and online

## WATER MIXTURE

| Ingredient | Metric | Weight | Volume | Baker's % |
|---|---|---|---|---|
| Water | 2 L | 4 lb, 6 oz | 2 L | n/a |
| Honey or corn syrup | 180 g | 6.3 oz | 160 ml | n/a |

## The CHEWY Bagel

Bagel aficionados often will favor a bagel that is a little on the chewy side, which is the result of using a combination of high-gluten flour and bread flour in the formula. High-gluten flour encourages more of the protein to build into its weblike structure, resulting in a more elastic, or extensible, dough and a chewier bagel. If you prefer your bagels to be less chewy or you are afraid your mixer might not be able to handle the extra strength of this dough, then by all means use bread flour instead, although it may help to hold back about 20 grams of water from the original formula.

It is always important to "listen to your equipment." It is normal for the mixer to strain a bit while mixing this bread formula, but smoke billowing out from the motor is not!

5. Dividing the bagel dough and starting to shape

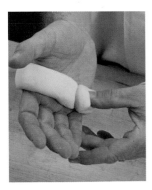

6a. Sealing the ends of the bagel

6b. Rolling the ring to compress the ends together

### 1. Mise en Place

Prepare and scale all ingredients.

**ADDITIONAL SPECIAL EQUIPMENT**
Large plastic bag
Large shallow stockpot
Slotted spoon

### 2. Mixing

Place the bread flour, high-gluten flour, water, instant yeast, salt, and diastatic malt into the bowl of a stand mixer and mix on low speed for approximately 4 minutes.

After the ingredients have been incorporated, increase the mixing speed to medium and mix for an additional 2 to 4 minutes. (If the machine is straining, a couple of squirts of water from a spray bottle into the bowl can help.)

### 3. Fermentation

The bagel formula is unique in that the dough does not go through a proper bulk fermentation cycle. Instead the dough is divided immediately after being mixed, shaped, and then allowed to ferment overnight in the refrigerator.

### 4. Stretch and Folds/Degassing

Due to the tightness and stiffness of this dough, it does not benefit from a stretch-and-fold cycle.

### 5. Dividing

Place the dough on a nonfloured surface and cover with a plastic bag so the dough does not dry out.

Using a scale and dough divider or scraper, divide into 3.8-ounce (110-gram) portions. To prevent drying, cover the bulk portion with plastic wrap as you divide.

### 6. Preshaping/Shaping

Take a unit and roll it out, using your hands on a floured surface to form a log approximately ¾ inch (2 cm) thick and 10 inches (25 cm) long, making the ends just a bit thicker that the centre, like a dog's bone.

Make a ring with the dough around your hand and tack the ends together, using a bit of pinching pressure.

With the seam side down, gently press your palm down on the table and roll the dough to compress the ends together. The seam will still be visible but secure. It is normal for this part of the bagel to be slightly thinner than the rest, but try to keep it as uniform as possible while still compressing the ends together.

### 7. Final Proof

Place the bagels on a parchment-lined sheet pan coated with nonstick cooking spray. Place the sheet pan inside a plastic bag, creating a tent over the bagels. Use plastic wrap if a bag is not available. Place in the refrigerator overnight.

### 8. Scoring

Bagel dough is a tightly structured dough, so there is no need to provide release points through scoring. Instead, it needs to be boiled in a water mixture so as to develop the proper flavour characteristics.

Preheat the oven at least 30 minutes prior to baking to 420°F (215°C, gas mark 6). If the oven has a convection mode, use it at 400°F (200°C, gas mark 6).

Combine the water and honey in a large stockpot and bring to a boil. Corn syrup may be substituted for the honey, although there will be a slight difference in the flavour. If any impurities from the honey rise to the top, skim them off with a fine sieve.

Remove the bagels from the refrigerator and place them, 4 to 6 at a time, into the boiling water for 10 to 15 seconds. Turn them over and boil for another 10 to 15 seconds. The bagels should float. If they do not, they have not fully proofed, so let the remaining unboiled bagels rest at room temperature for another 30 minutes before boiling.

Place on cooling rack to drip dry. If toppings such as poppy seeds, sunflower seeds, or sesame seeds are desired, dip the tops of the bagels into piles of the toppings while the bagels still are sticky and moist. If the seeds do not stick, the bagel is either too wet or has dried too long.

### 9. Baking

Place the bagels on a parchment-lined sheet pan and bake (preferably in a convection oven) for 15 to 20 minutes, or until the desired colour is achieved. The honey in the water mixture provides a golden shine and a rich brown colour.

8a. Removing the boiled bagel with a slotted spoon

8b. Dip the bagels into seeds to add variation.

9. The bagels are ready to bake.

### 10. Cooling/Storage

Let the bagels cool on a rack for a minimum of 30 minutes before eating. Bagels are easy to store and they keep soft when kept in plastic food storage bags for a day or two. To store longer, place the bagels in freezer bags and freeze for up to a month.

## VARIATION: **Bagel Bites and Logs**

| | |
|---|---|
| SHAPING AND BAKING: | **Easy** |
| YIELD: | **Approximately twenty-four 5-inch (13 cm) logs or 120 bites** |

MAKING LOGS OR BITES from bagel dough offers all the satisfaction of a bagel without the normal bagel size.

**Prepare Formula Six (Bagel Dough) through step 6, Preshaping/Shaping** (see pages 100–103), except do not form bagels into rings.

After rolling the dough into the 10-inch (25 cm) logs, divide them in half for Bagel Logs or into 1-inch (2.5 cm) pieces for Bagel Bites.

**Follow the remaining steps in the main Bagel Dough formula:**

Place on a parchment-lined sheet pan coated with nonstick cooking spray.

Place the sheet pan inside a plastic bag, creating a tent over the dough, and place in the refrigerator overnight.

Preheat the oven at least 30 minutes prior to baking to 420°F (215°C, gas mark 6). If the oven has a convection mode, use it at 400°C (200°C, gas mark 6). While waiting for the oven to heat up, combine the water and honey together in a large stockpot and bring to a boil.

Take the bites or logs and place them in the boiling water for 10 to 15 seconds. Turn them over and let boil for another 10 to 15 seconds.

Place on cooling rack to drip dry. If desired, dip into piles of seeds while the bagels still are sticky and moist from boiling.

Place on a parchment-lined sheet pan and bake (preferably in a convection oven) for 15 to 20 minutes, or until desired colour is achieved.

The dough is divided to make the bites and logs.

# VARIATION: Bialy

SHAPING AND BAKING: **Easy**

YIELD: **12 bialys**

A **BIALY IS** very similar to a bagel, but instead of being boiled and then baked, it is simply baked. Instead of a hole, it has a slight depression that is filled with diced onions and other ingredients, which can include garlic, poppy seeds, and bread crumbs.

Onion Filling: See Savoury Inspirations (page 157).

**Prepare Formula Six (Bagel Dough) through step 5, Dividing.** (See pages 100–102)

### 6. Preshaping/Shaping

Take each unit and gently shape into a round form.

### 7. Final Proof

Place on a parchment-lined sheet pan coated with non-stick cooking spray or dusted with flour, cover with a "plastic tent" as with bagels, and place in the refrigerator overnight.

### 8. Scoring

As with bagels, bialys need no scoring, but they do need to be formed to hold the filling. Preheat the oven to 440°F (227°C, gas mark 8), using a convection mode if available at 420°F (215°C, gas mark 6). With well-floured hands, take each unit and gently form a depression either by holding the dough and pressing the centre thinner or by pressing the centre down and out on a table surface. There should be a distinct rim around the outer edge of the bialy.

### 9. Baking

Take a portion of the cooled onion mixture and fill the centre depression of the bialy, spreading it out evenly.

Place bialys on a parchment-lined sheet pan and put in the oven for 15 to 20 minutes. Bialys are done when the crust of the outer rim is firm and you can detect some golden colour.

8. Use your hands to press out the rimmed disks.

9. Fill the centre of the bialy with the onion mixture.

### 10. Cooling/Storage

Remove from the oven and place the baked bialys on cooling racks. Allow to cool and serve either warm or at room temperature.

Because of the onion filling, bialys are best enjoyed fresh or by the next day. To store overnight, place in a container and cover with plastic to refrigerate. A quick warm-up in the toaster oven reheats the bialys nicely.

# FORMULA SEVEN: Pain de Mie

PAIN DE MIE is a white sandwich bread traditionally baked in a specially designed pan with a sliding lid, although regular bread pans can also be used. Its name translates from French to "crumb bread," referring to its denser and finer crumb structure with a comparatively tender crust. This bread contains more sugar than most French breads (but certainly not nearly as much as mainstream commercial sandwich bread!) and contains some fat as well, so it keeps longer and freezes well. Pain de mie has a very neutral flavour and is therefore traditionally used as a canvas for other accompanying flavours, such as in tea sandwiches and canapés.

## FINAL DOUGH

| Ingredient | Metric | Weight | Volume | Baker's % |
|---|---|---|---|---|
| Bread flour | 666 g | 1 lb, 7.3 oz | | 100 |
| Salt | 16 g | 0.5 oz | 1¼ tsp | 2.4 |
| Sugar | 26 g | 0.9 oz | 1¾ tsp | 3.9 |
| Instant yeast (preferably osmotolerant) | 7 g | 0.24 oz | 2 tsp | 1 |
| Whole milk | 400 g | 14.1 oz | 415 ml | 60 |
| Butter, softened | 120 g | 4.2 oz | | 18 |

## The PULLMAN Loaf

The American equivalent of pain de mie is known as Pullman bread, which got its name from the association to the Pullman railroad cars of the early 1900s, although there is some debate on how the name was actually derived. Some sources indicate that the bread and the lidded pans were developed as a space-saving device for use in the tightly constricted railcar kitchens. Others claim that the only connection between the bread and the railcar, besides its name, is its long, rectangular shape. Either way, the Pullman loaf eventually evolved into an easily recognizable mainstream bread style.

## 1. Mise en Place

Prepare and scale all ingredients

**ADDITIONAL SPECIAL EQUIPMENT**
> 1 lidded Pullman loaf pan 13 x 4 x 4 inches
> (33 x 10 x 10 cm) *or*
> 2 bread loaf pans 8½ x 4½ x 2½ inches
> (22 x 11 x 6 cm)

## 2. Mixing

In the bowl of a stand mixer with a dough hook attachment, combine the bread flour, salt, sugar, instant yeast, and whole milk and mix on low speed for about 4 minutes.

After the ingredients have been incorporated, increase to medium speed and add half of the softened butter. Mix for 1 minute.

Add the remaining softened butter and mix for an additional 5 minutes. Initially the sound of the butter slapping against the wall of the bowl will be clearly audible, but as the mixing time progresses this sound should diminish. By the end of the 5 minutes, the butter should be completely and evenly incorporated into the dough.

3. The mixed pain de mie ready to ferment

## 3. Fermentation

Take the dough out of the mixing bowl and place in a proofing container coated with nonstick cooking spray. The ideal dough temperature would be 78°F (26°C).

Cover the container with a lid or plastic wrap and allow the dough to ferment for 45 minutes.

## 4. Stretch and Folds/Degassing

After the dough ferments for 45 minutes, give it one series of stretch and folds (see page 32), return to the proofing container, and allow to rest for an additional 45 minutes.

## 5. Dividing

Turn out the dough onto a floured surface. Using a scale and dough divider, divide the dough mass in half.

6. Twisting the dough ensures a consistent crumb structure.

## 6. Preshaping/Shaping

Preheat the oven to 375°F (190°C, gas mark 5). No baking stone or steaming tray is necessary.

Preshape each unit into a log roll. If using a Pullman pan, use your hands to shape each log like a baguette to 24 to 26 inches (60 to 65 cm), but avoid tapering the ends. If using regular bread pans, shape each piece into an oval, leaving the ends blunt (not pointed).

If using a Pullman pan, gently twist the rolled pieces to form a loose spiral. This ensures the bread will yield a consistent crumb structure.

If using a Pullman pan, coat the pan and lid with nonstick cooking spray. Place the loaf gently into the pan. The dough should come about halfway up the sides of the pan. Slide the lid on the pan, leaving about a 1-inch (2.5 cm) opening at one end so you may check the progress of the dough. If using regular loaf pans, coat the pans with cooking spray and place the preshaped dough into the pans.

### 7. Final Proof

Let the dough proof for 45 minutes to 1 hour. The dough should rise to just about ½ inch (1 cm) below the lid. If using a Pullman pan, be sure to close the lid before baking.

### 8. Scoring

The pain de mie does not need scoring. The outward energy thrust during baking will force the dough to fill the entire interior of the Pullman pan and then back in, creating the desired denser, tighter crumb structure.

### 9. Baking

Place the loaf pan in the centre of the oven and bake for 30 minutes.

After 30 minutes of baking, remove the lids from the pans and return the loaves to the oven. Reduce the oven temperature to 350°F (180°C, gas mark 4) and bake for another 15 minutes.

Take the bread from the oven and remove it from the pan. Place it back into the oven directly on the oven rack for another 3 to 5 minutes, to ensure even browning.

### 10. Cooling/Storage

Place the bread on a wire rack to cool and wait preferably at least 6 hours before cutting.

This bread keeps a week if well wrapped in plastic. To freeze, wrap tightly in several layers of plastic wrap and place in the freezer for up to 2 months.

7. Loaves proofing in Pullman pans

## WHOLE WHEAT Variation

Baking bread with whole wheat flour can be challenging: The sharp edges of the bran in the flour actually cut into the gluten structure. Luckily, it is easy to substitute 20 percent of the bread flour with whole wheat flour, adding more flavour, texture, and nutrients to the bread. You can try this approach with the other formulas in this book—just be aware that a bit more water may need to be added.

# VARIATION:
# Cinnamon Spice Swirl Bread

SHAPING AND BAKING: **Medium**

YIELD: **1 loaf**

THERE IS SOMETHING innately comforting about Cinnamon Spice Swirl Bread: the taste of cinnamon that triggers warm memories from childhood, or the anticipation as the smell of the toasting bread wafts into the kitchen air.

Prepare the Cinnamon Spice Mix (see page 156 for formula) by combining all the ingredients in a bowl and mixing well. This can be made ahead of time and stored in an airtight container.

**Prepare Formula Seven (Pain de Mie) through step 4, Stretch and Folds/Degassing.** (See pages 106–108.)

---

**ADDITIONAL SPECIAL EQUIPMENT**

Rolling pin

---

## 5. Dividing

If you are using a long Pullman pan, no dividing is necessary. If you choose to use regular loaf pans, this formula yields 2 loaves, so divide the dough mass into 2 equal units with a scale and dough divider.

## 6. Preshaping/Shaping

Preheat the oven to 375˚F (190˚C, gas mark 5). A baking stone and steaming tray are not necessary.

On a floured surface, roll out the dough with a rolling pin to about 13 inches (33 cm) in one direction (8 inches [20 cm] if using regular bread pans).

Turn the dough 90˚ and roll out the other direction to about 18 inches (46 cm) (12 inches [30 cm] if using regular bread pans). Keep the piece as rectangular as possible. Spread the cinnamon spice mixture onto the surface of the dough.

Take the short end of the dough and roll up tightly like a jelly roll, sealing the seam at the end.

Place into a Pullman pan coated with nonstick cooking spray and replace the lid, keeping it open about 1 inch (2.5 cm) at the end to check the proofing progress. If you are using regular bread pans, coat them with nonstick cooking spray and gently place the dough into them and cover lightly with plastic wrap.

6a. Rolling up the Cinnamon Spice Swirl Bread

### 7. Final Proof

Allow the dough to rest and proof for 1 to 1¼ hours. The dough should rise to about ½ inch (1 cm) just under the lid of the pan.

**Follow the remaining steps of the Pain de Mie.**
Place the loaf pan in the centre of the oven and let bake for 30 minutes. After 30 minutes of baking, remove the lids from the pans and return the loaves to the oven. Reduce the oven temperature to 350°F (180°C, gas mark 4) and bake for another 15 minutes.

Take the bread from the oven and remove it from the pan. Place it back into the oven directly on the oven rack for another 3 to 5 minutes to ensure even browning.

Place the bread on a wire rack to cool and wait preferably at least 6 hours before cutting.

6b. Placing the rolled-up dough into the oiled pan

## VARIATION: **Raisin Rolls**

SHAPING AND BAKING. **Easy**

YIELD: **18 rolls**

THESE RAISIN ROLLS are a quick way to add flavour and variety to the Pain de Mie main formula. Try making a smaller loaf of the pain de mie. You'll still have enough dough to make 6 to 9 rolls for dinner or to freeze for later use.

**Prepare Formula Seven (Pain de Mie) through step 4, Stretch and Folds/Degassing** (see pages 106–108), adding 140 g (4.9 ounces) of golden raisins to the dough after the butter is mixed in in step 2. Mix on low speed until the raisins are completely incorporated. Also prepare the cinnamon spice mix from the previous variation (see page 156).

> **ADDITIONAL SPECIAL EQUIPMENT**
> Parchment-lined sheet pan
> Water spray bottle

6. The raisin rolls ready to proof

9. The rolls are sprinkled with the cinnamon spice mixture.

### 5. Dividing

Using a scale and a dough divider, section off the dough into 12 units (90 grams [3.2 ounces] each).

### 6. Preshaping/Shaping

Preheat the oven to 375°F (190°C, gas mark 5). A baking stone and steaming tray are not necessary.

Shape the dough into round units and place on a parchment-lined sheet pan.

### 7. Final Proof

Cover the sheet pan with plastic wrap and let proof until the rolls double in size.

### 8. Scoring

The rolls do not need to be scored.

### 9. Baking

Just before baking, mist the tops of the rolls with water from the spray bottle and sprinkle the tops liberally with the cinnamon spice mixture.

Place the sheet pan into the oven and bake for 20 to 24 minutes.

### 10. Cooling/Storage

Remove from the oven and let cool in the sheet pan on the cooling rack.

For a sweeter alternative, drizzle some sugar glaze (see page 153) over the cooled rolls. Store in a plastic food storage bag for 4 to 5 days or wrap tightly in plastic and freeze for up to a month.

## VARIATION: **Picnic Rolls**

SHAPING AND BAKING: **Easy**

YIELD: **12 sandwich or hot-dog rolls**

FRESH ROLLS ARE an unexpected but most welcome surprise at any picnic gathering. Somehow a homemade roll makes even the most delicious hamburger (or veggie burger!) taste even better. Yes, it does take a bit more effort than tossing a bag into the shopping cart, but the accolades you will receive will be well worth it.

**Prepare Formula Seven (Pain de Mie) through step 4, Stretch and Folds/Degassing.** (See pages 106–108.)

> **ADDITIONAL SPECIAL EQUIPMENT**
> Parchment-lined sheet pan
> Pastry brush

### 5. Dividing

Using a scale and dough divider, section off 90-gram (3.2 ounce) portions of dough.

### 6. Preshaping/Shaping

Preheat the oven to 385°F (196°C, gas mark 6).

Hot-dog rolls should be preshaped into log forms, and sandwich rolls should be preshaped round. Cover them with plastic and let them rest for about 20 minutes.

For final shaping of the hot-dog rolls, gently degas the rolls and roll up the dough to shape like a mini baguette (see Step 6 photos in Formula One, Baguette Dough, pages 61–62). Place seam side down on a parchment-lined sheet pan and brush with egg wash (see page 153). For the final shaping of the sandwich rolls, gently reround the rolls and place on the parchment-lined sheet pan.

### 7. Final Proof

Cover the dough with plastic and let it proof for about 45 minutes at room temperature.

Uncover the dough and degas it by pressing down with the palm of your hand. Brush the tops of the rolls with an egg wash and sprinkle with sesame or poppy seeds if desired. Let them sit for another 10 minutes before baking.

### 8. Scoring

The sandwich rolls do not need to be scored.

### 9. Baking

Place into the oven and bake for 20 to 25 minutes. The rolls should have a golden brown crust and a soft body when squeezed.

### 10. Cooling/Storage

Remove from the oven and place on a cooling rack to cool. Before serving, take a sharp serrated knife and carefully cut the sandwich rolls in half and the hot-dog rolls about halfway through. These rolls keep fresh when stored in plastic for 3 or 4 days. Otherwise, wrap tightly in plastic and freeze for 1 to 2 months.

7. Degassing the sandwich rolls and applying egg wash

## SEEDS: Raw or Roasted?

Raw seeds or nuts can coat the outside of a bread (such as the Picnic Rolls, page 112). The direct heat applied during baking roasts the coating and enhances their rich flavor. If seeds or nuts are incorporated into the dough (such as the Whole Wheat Bread, page 78), it's best to roast them beforehand. Spread the seeds or nuts evenly on a sheet pan and roast for 6–9 minutes at 375°F (190°C, gas mark 5). Let the seeds cool completely.

# FORMULA EIGHT: Challah Dough

**CHALLAH IS A STUNNING** braided bread that is certain to capture everyone's attention as it is brought to the table to serve. Traditionally reserved for eating on the Sabbath, this historically Jewish bread is now enjoyed more liberally in the United States and is available every day of the week. There are many different ways to braid a challah loaf, ranging from the simple to more complex, with the more complicated versions used to commemorate special occasions.

## SPONGE

| Ingredient | Metric | Weight | Volume | Baker's % |
|---|---|---|---|---|
| Bread flour | 172 g | 6 oz | | 100 |
| Water, 75°F (24°C) | 110 g | 3.8 oz | 120 ml | 59.5 |
| Instant yeast, preferably osmotolerant | 11 g | 0.4 oz | Scant 4 tsp | 6.8 |

Prepare the sponge about 30 minutes before mixing the final dough. Combine the ingredients in the bowl of a stand mixer, mix together on low speed until incorporated, and cover the mixing bowl with plastic wrap. The sponge should develop rather quickly; when it has doubled in size it is ready to use. While you are waiting for the sponge to develop, you can be scaling your ingredients for the final dough.

## FINAL DOUGH

| Ingredient | Metric | Weight | Volume | Baker's % |
|---|---|---|---|---|
| Bread flour | 518 g | 1 pound, 2.2 oz | | 100 |
| Sugar | 78 g | 2.7 oz | | 15 |
| Salt | 14 g | 0.5 oz | 2 tsp | 2.7 |
| Honey | 41 g | 1.4 oz | 40 ml | 7.9 |
| Water, 70°F (21°C) | 30 g | 1.1 oz | 30 ml | 5.7 |
| Whole eggs | 150 g | 5.2 oz | 3 eggs | 28.9 |
| Egg yolks | 50 g | 1.7 oz | 2 yolks | 9.6 |
| Vegetable oil | 64 g | 2.2 oz | 65 ml | 12.3 |
| Sponge | All of it | All of it | All of it | 56.5 |

3. Take the dough out of the mixing bowl and place it in the proofing container.

### 1. Mise en Place

Prepare and scale all ingredients.

### 2. Mixing

In a stand mixer with a dough hook, combine all ingredients and mix on low speed for about 8 minutes. Increase to a medium speed and mix for an additional 8 minutes. Watch the mixer to make sure it does not "walk".

### 3. Fermentation

Place the dough in a proofing container coated with nonstick cooking spray, with room for the dough to double in size. Test the internal temperature of the dough; it should be between 75°F and 78°F (24°C and 26°C). Cover with a lid or plastic wrap and let the dough rest at room temperature for 1¼ hours or until it doubles in size.

### 4. Stretch and Folds/Degassing

This dough does not benefit from a stretch and fold.

### 5. Dividing

Using a scale and dough divider, divide the dough evenly into units. Weights will depend on the number of strands the braid will have: 110 grams (3.3 ounces) for a 3-strand braid, 115 grams (4 ounces) for a 5-strand braid.

### 6. Preshaping/Shaping

Using your hands, shape the units into rounds. Cover them lightly with plastic wrap and let them rest for about 20 minutes. After resting, roll the rounds into 12- to 18-inch (30 to 46 cm) strands. The strands should be slightly thicker in the middle and tapered at the ends. If the dough feels a bit dry, do not hesitate to spray it with water from a spray bottle.

## A CHALLAH WREATH

After you have made your 3-strand braid, you can coil it up for a quick change in shape. Pinch the ends in to the body of the wreath to secure them and brush the tops with egg wash.

## ROLLING OUT Strands

When dough is rolled into strands, sometimes it needs time to relax. Roll one strand until it starts to feel tight, then set it aside and roll the next strand. Continue rolling out all strands, keeping them in the order that they were rolled. Return to the first strand and roll it out again. The second time around the dough will be bit more relaxed and will extend even further. Repeat until the desired length is reached.

## 3-STRAND BRAIDING TECHNIQUE

The complete 3-strand braid

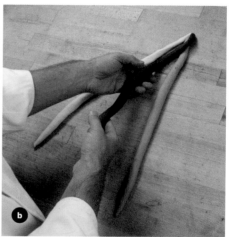

Now the fun begins: braiding! Illustrated are 3-strand and 5-strand braiding sequences, along with a double-decker version. *Note: The dough has been coloured to create a visual marker to follow throughout each sequence. The actual dough will not have any colour.*

For a 3-strand braid, lay 3 strands vertically in front of you on the table, with the top ends connected and slightly pressed together **(a)**.

Take the right-side strand and cross it leftward over the centre strand. It should now occupy the centre position **(b)**.

Take the left-side strand and cross it rightward over the centre strand. Now it should occupy the centre position **(c)**.

Repeat this sequence **(d)** until the braid is finished and seal the bottom ends together. Gently tuck under the ends of the braid just a little bit to give it a cleaner, more finished look.

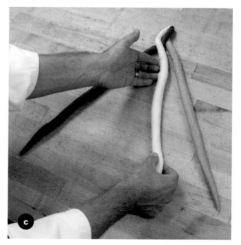

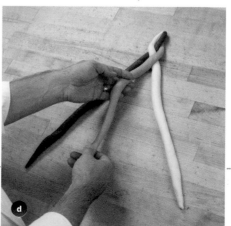

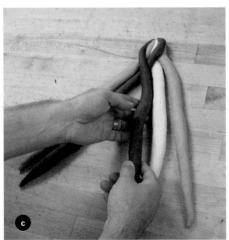

## 5-STRAND BRAIDING TECHNIQUE

The complete 5-strand braid

For a 5-strand braid (a decorative braid that looks more complicated than it is), connect 5 strands at the top and gently fan them out, grouping 2 strands on the left and 3 strands on the right **(a)**.

Take the strand on the far right and cross it over 2 strands to occupy the centre position **(b)**.

Take the strand on the far left and cross it over 2 strands to occupy the centre position **(c)**.

Repeat this sequence **(d)** until the braid is finished and seal the bottom ends together. Gently tuck under the ends of the braid just a little bit to give it a cleaner, more finished look.

For a double-decker braid (two braids together for special occasions), braid a 3-strand and a 5-strand braid, the 3-strand being slightly smaller. Sprinkle a bit of flour down the centre line of the 5-strand braid and use a wooden dowel to roll out an indentation for the 3-strand braid to be placed into. This will take a few tries, since the dough needs some time to relax after the braiding.

Brush any excess flour away from the 5-strand braid, then lay the 3-strand braid into the bed.

## 7. Final Proof

Place the breads onto a parchment-lined sheet pan. Spray each braid with a light mist of water and cover with plastic wrap. Let proof at room temperature for 60 to 75 minutes. The braided loaf should double before baking.

Preheat the oven to 350°F (180°C, gas mark 4) about 30 minutes before baking. If there is a convection mode, use it at 330°F (165°C, gas mark 3).

## 8. Scoring

This bread does not need any scoring. The tension will release gently where the braided strands overlap.

## 9. Baking

Brush the top of the braid with egg wash (see page 153), and sprinkle with poppy or sesame seeds if desired.

Place the sheet pan with the challah in the oven and bake. The time will vary depending on the size of the braid; larger units will need at least 30 minutes of baking, and smaller units will need at least 20 minutes. If the dough seems to be browning too quickly, reduce the oven temperature by 20°F (11°C).

## 10. Cooling/Storage

Remove from the oven and sheet pan and allow to cool completely on a wire rack. Enjoy the challah within a day or two, wrapping it in plastic to prevent drying. To freeze, wrap tightly in plastic wrap and freeze for up to 2 weeks.

Press a rolling pin into a 5-strand braid.

The complete double-decker braid

## Making CLARIFIED BUTTER

Place a stick of unsalted butter in a small saucepan and melt over low heat. Allow to simmer for 20 to 30 minutes until all the milk solids have separated out of the liquid. Skim off the foam at the top with a spoon, then pour the butter through a strainer to remove the solids. Store this clarified butter in the refrigerator until ready to use.

## Orange Aniseed Wheels

SHAPING AND BAKING: **Easy**

YIELD: **12 wheels**

THE AROMATIC ORANGE BLOSSOM water and candied orange peel combined with the delicate flavour of anise produce one of the most unique and delicious flavour combinations possible. Don't let the anise scare you: Many people who claim anise as one of their least favourite flavours are surprised at how subtle it is when complemented by the tones of the orange.

| Ingredient | Metric | Weight | Volume |
|---|---|---|---|
| Orange blossom water | 29 g | 1 oz | 30 ml |
| Aniseeds | 7 g | 0.24 oz | 2 tsp |
| Candied orange peel | 82 g | 2.8 oz | |

**Prepare Formula 8 (Challah Dough) through step 4, Stretch and Folds/Degassing** (see pages 114–116), adding the above ingredients on first speed after the dough has developed a full gluten window.

### 5. Dividing

Divide the dough into 3.5 ounce (100-gram) units and work into rounds.

### 6. Preshaping/Shaping

Let rest for 20 minutes, then gently work round again and press the dough down flat with the palm of your hand. Using a bench scraper or knife, cut 5 slits into the outside rim of the roll, and place on a parchment-lined sheet pan.

6. Use a bench knife to make the radiating cuts into the wheel.

### 7. Final Proof

Preheat the oven to 360°F (182°C, gas mark 4). A baking stone or steaming tray is not necessary. Cover the dough with plastic wrap and let proof for about 45 minutes. It should approximately double in size.

### 8. Scoring

No scoring is necessary; the cuts in the wheels will suffice.

### 9. Baking

Bake at 360°F (182°C, gas mark 4) for 10 to 14 minutes until golden brown. After baking, brush the tops with melted butter. Clarified butter (see page 120) will provide a longer shelf life.

9. Brush the tops with clarified butter.

### 10. Cooling/Storage

Toss the wheels in coarse granulated sugar for some sweet texture and place on a wire rack to cool. These are best if consumed by the following day; the sugar coating does not make them a good candidate for freezing.

# VARIATION: **Knotted Rolls**

SHAPING AND BAKING: **Easy/Medium**

YIELD: **18 rolls**

- - - - - - - - - - - - - - - - - - - - - - - - - - - - - - - - - - - - -

**WHEN A DOUGH** braids as easily as this one does, it is nice to take advantage of that in a smaller scale. These knotted rolls are like jewels in the breadbasket.

**Prepare Formula 8 (Challah Dough) through to step 5, Dividing** (see pages 114–116), except section off the dough into 3.5-ounce (100-gram) units.

### 6. Preshaping/Shaping

**For a fleur de lis:** On a surface, roll out a unit to about 16 inches (40 cm) long, leaving it slightly thicker in the middle and tapering the ends. Create a top loop in the centre by crossing the strand over itself, making sure to keep the loop open.

Create the side loops by bringing the ends of the strands up and back around over themselves. Twist the remaining dough strands together, creating a downward spiral to form the "stem."

**For a faux braid:** On a floured surface, roll out the unit to about 16 inches (40 cm), keeping it uniform in width. Place one end in the middle of the strand and gently pull to elongate into an oval, bringing the remaining half of the dough straight down on the outer right side.

Tuck the long end under the end at the top of the oval and bring it across to the left side. Take the bottom of the oval with your fingers and twist it over to the right, creating a smaller loop at the bottom. Take the remaining dough end and slide it up from the bottom through the twisted loop. Cut off any excess dough with a knife or pair of scissors.

Follow the remaining step in the Challah main formula. Place the knotted rolls onto a parchment-lined sheet pan. Spray with a light mist of water and cover with plastic wrap. Let proof at room temperature for 30 to 45 minutes.

Preheat the oven to 350°F (180°C, gas mark 4) about 30 minutes before baking. If there is a convection mode, use it at 330°F (165°C, gas mark 3). Brush the tops with egg wash and sprinkle with pearl sugar or cinnamon sugar. For unsweetened rolls, use poppy or sesame seeds, or just leave them plain. Place the sheet pan with the knotted rolls in the oven and bake for 10 to 15 minutes. Remove from the oven and sheet pan and allow to cool completely on a wire rack.

## FORMULA NINE: Brioche Dough

BRIOCHE IS LOVINGLY REFERRED to as the cousin of the croissant. Typically found adorning many breakfast tables throughout France, the brioche boasts a soft texture and derives its delectable flavour from its rich ingredients: eggs, butter, and a bit of sugar. Brioche is one of the most basic, yet one of the most versatile, enriched doughs and should be considered a staple in every baker's repertoire. It can be made in a variety of shapes and sizes, but its most famous shape is the *brioche à tête*, a small fluted roll with a "head" on top.

| Ingredient | Metric | Weight | Volume | Baker's % |
| --- | --- | --- | --- | --- |
| Milk | 185 g | 6.5 oz | 180 ml | 42 |
| Whole egg | 1 egg | 1 egg | 1 egg | 11 |
| Egg yolk* | 1 yolk | 1 yolk | 1 yolk | 5.5 |
| Lemon zest | ¼ lemon | ¼ lemon | ¼ lemon | n/a |
| Bread flour | 440 g | 15.5 oz | | 100 |
| Granulated sugar | 45 g | 1.5 oz | | 10.2 |
| Instant yeast, preferably osmotolerant | 12 g | 0.4 oz | 3¾ tsp | 2.7 |
| Salt | 7 g | 0.2 oz | 1 tsp | 1.6 |
| Unsalted butter, cold | 165 g | 5.8 oz | | 37.5 |

*Reserve the egg white in case the dough is too dry (see step 2).

2a. Make the butter pliable with a rolling pin.

2b. The sticky sides of the bowl indicate that the butter has not yet fully incorporated into the dough.

## 1. Mise en Place

Prepare and scale all ingredients.

**ADDITIONAL SPECIAL EQUIPMENT**
Lemon zester
Brioche tins or muffin tins

## 2. Mixing

Put the milk, egg, and egg yolk together in the bowl of a stand mixer. Zest the lemon into the wet ingredients.

In a separate bowl, combine the bread flour, granulated sugar, instant yeast, and salt. Pour the dry ingredients into the stand mixer bowl with the wet ingredients.

Mix together with a dough hook attachment on a low speed for about 4 minutes, until the dough comes together in a homogenous mass, otherwise known as the cleanup stage (see page 31). If the dough seems to be too dry, you can add some or all of the egg white left over from the egg separated to get the egg yolk.

While these ingredients are mixing, make the butter pliable by hammering it with a rolling pin. The butter should become soft and achieve a consistency similar to children's play dough.

Increase to medium speed and after the dough has mixed about 1 minute, slowly add the butter in 4 stages to the mixture. As soon as you add the first stage of butter, the dough will start to make a sticky slapping sound against the wall of the mixer. Do not add the next stage of butter until this sound diminishes and the butter is completely incorporated into the dough. Look to see that the sides of the inside of the bowl are almost completely clean before adding the next stage of butter.

2c. Testing the dough with a gluten window: an underdeveloped dough on the right and a properly developed dough on the left. (See page 31.)

Continue mixing on medium speed until the dough is fully developed and has a good gluten window, anywhere from 10 to 20 minutes, depending on the mixer. Do not leave the mixer unattended, as the vibration may cause the mixer to move. Also, if you notice that your mixer is overheating, turn it off and give it a break. Cover the bowl with plastic wrap if you need to stop mixing for a while.

### 3. Fermentation

Shape the dough round. Wrap loosely with plastic and place in the freezer for at least 6 hours. At this stage, the dough can be stored in the freezer for up to 3 weeks, so feel free to divide it into smaller sections for easier future use.

Remove the dough from the freezer the night before use and place in the refrigerator for 12 hours.

### 4. Stretch and Folds/Degassing

This dough does not benefit from a stretch-and-fold sequence.

### 5. Dividing

Take the dough out of the refrigerator and let it sit at room temperature for about 30 minutes. Using a scale and dough divider, section off into 10 equal pieces (90 grams [3.2 ounces] each).

## The Need to FREEZE

You may be curious about why this dough needs to be frozen and cannot just be put into the refrigerator to rest. Because the dough is mixed intensively, a lot of strength and heat are generated in the dough. The dough needs the long time to relax so that it can be worked, but its fermentation cycle needs to be slowed down quickly so that it doesn't develop too fast. Putting it in the freezer ensures a quick cooldown and provides an intermediate storage solution for dough that won't be used right away.

5. Dividing the portions for the brioches.

6a. Gently roll with the edge of your hand to create the brioche neck.

6b. Elongate the neck with your fingers.

6c. Make a hole in the dough with your thumbs.

6d. Push the head up through the hole.

7. Cover the dough with a plastic tent to proof.

## 6. Preshaping/Shaping

Coat the brioche forms or muffin tins with nonstick cooking spray.

First, preshape the units into rounds. Then, using a rolling motion with the edge of your hand, create a "neck" about one-third of the way down.

Continue to gently roll the dough and provide more downward pressure, elongating the neck until it is about 3 fingers wide.

Using your thumbs, make a hole in the "body" part of the dough that is large enough for the head and neck to pass through.

Gently push the heads through the holes and place into the fluted brioche forms or muffin tins.

## 7. Final Proof

Place the forms on a sheet pan and cover with plastic, tenting it over the brioches so that the plastic does not touch the dough. Place 4 tall drinking glasses at the outside of each sheet pan corner to help support the plastic wrap, if necessary. Let the dough proof at room temperature for 1 to 2 hours, until the dough has doubled in size.

Preheat oven to 365°F (185°C, gas mark 4) about 30 minutes before baking. A baking stone and steaming tray are not necessary. If the oven has a convection mode, use it at 345°F (174°C, gas mark 3).

### 8. Scoring

Brioches do not need to be scored.

### 9. Baking

After the final proof, brush the tops of the brioches with an egg wash (see page 153).

Place the sheet pan of brioche forms or muffin tins into the oven. Bake the brioches for 10 to 14 minutes, until a dark golden brown.

### 10. Cooling/Storing

Take the brioches out the oven and let them cool in the forms for about 5 minutes. Remove the brioches from the forms and continue to cool on a wire rack.

Individual brioches are difficult to freeze and are best when enjoyed the day they have been baked.

9. Brush the tops with an egg wash.

## BRIOCHE in a Pan

If you don't have the time to make individual brioches, you can still enjoy the delicate, buttery flavour of brioche baked in a bread pan. Simply divide some of the dough into 10 50-gram units (1.75 ounce), shape round, and place in 2 rows (rounds touching) in a 9 x 5-inch (23 x 13cm) loaf pan coated with nonstick cook-ing spray. Brush with an egg wash glaze before baking at 350˚F (180°C, gas mark 4) (330˚F with convection mode) for 25 to 30 minutes.

This variation of brioche will keep fresher longer and is good for making French toast and bread pudding.

# Sticky Bun Coffee Cake

| | |
|---|---|
| SHAPING AND BAKING: | **Easy** |
| YIELD: | **2 coffee cakes** |

WHO CAN RESIST a warm coffee cake, the glazed sugar rivulets flowing into small pools of sweetness? Not I, which is why I developed this formula. One of the great things about this coffee cake is that you can change the filling to fit your fancy: One day it can be pastry cream with mini chocolate chips and the next day it is hazelnut spread—or maybe you are just in the mood for a simple cinnamon sugar. It is a perfect item to serve at brunch and makes a great addition to a bake sale table. Whatever the occasion may be, this coffee cake is sure to please.

**Prepare Formula 9 (Brioche Dough) through step 4, Stretch and Folds/Degassing.** (See pages 124–127)

**ADDITIONAL SPECIAL EQUIPMENT**
Rolling pin
9-inch (23-cm) cake pan or springform
(3 inches [7.5 cm] high)

## 5. Dividing

Take the dough out of the refrigerator and let it sit at room temperature for about 30 minutes. While the dough is warming up, make your sugar glaze (see page 153) and filling (see pages 154–155).

Section off about one-quarter of the dough. This can be done visually without a scale.

## 6. Preshaping/Shaping

Take the piece sectioned off and, with a rolling pin, roll the dough out to ¼ inch (6 mm) thick.

Grease a 9-inch (23 cm) cake or springform pan and line the bottom with parchment paper. From the rolled dough, cut a circle the size of the pan and place in the bottom. Trim off any excess.

Add the trimmings to the remaining dough and, on a floured surface, roll it out into a 9 x 12-inch (23 x 30 cm) rectangle that is ¼ inch (6 mm) thick.

Spread the desired filling evenly onto the dough and gently roll up the long end like a jelly roll into a 12-inch (30 cm) long log.

Using a sharp knife, cut the log into 1½-inch (4-cm) sections and place on the bottom layer of dough in the cake pan. (If your cake pan is less than 3 inches [7.5 cm] high, cut the sections 1 inch [2.5 cm].) Leave a little space between the sections to allow room for rising during the proofing stage.

6a. After spreading the filling, roll the dough up.

## 7. Final Proof

Place the pan in a plastic bag and tent it over the coffee cake so that it does not touch the dough. Let the dough proof at room temperature for 1 to 2 hours.

Preheat the oven to 350°F (180°C, gas mark 4) about 30 minutes before baking, using the convection mode if one is available at 330°F (165°C, gas mark 3).

6b. Cut the dough sections and place into pan.

## 8. Scoring

This coffee cake does not need to be scored.

## 9. Baking

Place the pan in the oven and bake for 30 to 40 minutes until golden brown. You may want to place the pan on a parchment-lined sheet pan to catch any sugary drippings. Keep an eye on the temperature; you may have to lower it if the coffee cake is getting too dark.

## 10. Cooling/Storage

Take the pan from the oven, remove the coffee cake, and place on a wire rack. While still warm, brush the top with the sugar glaze. Serve warm or at room temperature. The coffee cake will keep a few days if wrapped carefully to prevent drying out. Freezing it is not recommended.

## VARIATION:
# Sweet Filled Brioches

SHAPING AND BAKING: **Medium**

YIELD: **12 filled brioches**

THESE SWEET FILLED BRIOCHES pair perfectly with tea or coffee. The fillings can be easily varied—try the apple filling dusted with cinnamon sugar or the raisin-date filling with an egg wash glaze. Be creative and experiment!

**Prepare Formula 9 (Brioche Dough) through step 4, Stretch and Folds/Degassing.** (See pages 124–127.)

**ADDITIONAL SPECIAL EQUIPMENT**
Rolling pin

### 5. Dividing

Prepare filling for the brioches (see pages 154–155). Hazelnut is shown. Take the dough out of the refrigerator and let it sit at room temperature for about 30 minutes.

Using a scale and dough divider, section out dough into 12 equal portions (2.6 ounces [75 grams]), keeping the portions square-shaped if possible.

### 6. Preshaping/Shaping

On a lightly floured surface, take each unit and roll out into a ¼-inch-thick, 3-inch square (6 mm thick, 7.5 cm square). Place 2 tablespoons (40 g) of the desired filling in the centre of the dough and pinch the top of the square closed. With the seam side down, gently work the filled dough into rounds.

### 7. Final Proof

Place the dough seam side down on a parchment-lined sheet pan and proof until doubled in size, 1 to 2 hours.

### 8. Scoring

These sweet filled brioches do not need scoring. Preheat the oven to 360°F (182°C, gas mark 4), using the convection mode at 340°F (171°C, gas mark 3) if available. While waiting for the brioche to proof, prepare the chocolate glaze (see page 153).

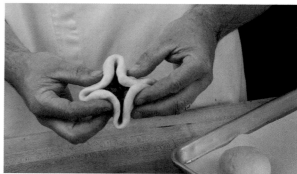

6. Fill dough and pinch seam closed.

9. Sprinkle powdered sugar on top for a nice effect.

### 9. Baking

Just before baking, spoon on the chocolate glaze to coat the tops of the brioche and sprinkle with toasted almonds, pearled sugar, or confectioners' sugar if desired.

Place a sheet pan in the oven and bake for about 15 minutes. The chocolate glaze will develop a slight crackle effect and the brioches will be a medium golden brown when done.

### 10. Cooling/Storage

Remove the brioches from the oven. Take the brioches off the sheet pan and let cool on a wire rack. These are best enjoyed the day of baking or the next morning. Unfortunately they do not freeze well, so eat them up or share them with friends and neighbors!

# FORMULA TEN: **Croissant Dough**

PERHAPS NO BREAD stirs the memory or imagination more than a croissant. One bite of the flaky, buttery layers and you are instantly transported through space and time to that little corner café in Paris, complete with a café au lait, a newspaper, and hours to lounge away the morning. How romantic! Ah yes, the power of the croissant—wake me when I am done dreaming.

The croissant *is* the quintessential breakfast pastry of France and is ingrained in the daily French culture as much as the baguette. It is a time-consuming labor of love, requiring more than just a few passes of the rolling pin. The key to a flaky croissant is successful lamination. This is the process of rolling and folding a dough encased in butter that creates thin, distinct, alternating layers of butter and dough. When baked, the moisture in the layers of butter create steam and act as the primary leavening agent in the croissant, puffing out to separate the layers of dough and creating that famously flaky texture so sought after in a croissant.

## FINAL DOUGH

| Ingredient | Metric | Weight | Volume | Baker's % |
|---|---|---|---|---|
| Bread flour | 690 g | 1 lb, 8.3 oz | | 100 |
| Whole milk | 310 g | 10.9 oz | 315 ml | 44.9 |
| Whole eggs | 100 g | 3.5 oz | 2 eggs | 14.4 |
| Granulated sugar | 81 g | 2.8 oz | | 11.7 |
| Salt | 13 g | 0.45 oz | 2 tsp | 1.8 |
| Instant yeast, preferably osmotolerant | 9 g | 0.3 oz | 2½ tsp | 1.3 |
| Unsalted butter | 19 g | 0.6 oz | | 2.7 |

## BUTTER BLOCK

| Ingredient | Metric | Weight | Volume | Baker's % |
|---|---|---|---|---|
| Unsalted butter, 83% butterfat | 330 g | 11.6 oz | | 47.8 |

## 1. Mise en Place

Prepare and scale all ingredients. Bring unsalted butter in Final Dough ingredients to room temperature (not the butter in the Butter Block).

## 2. Mixing

Bring all milk and eggs to 60°F (15°C), or a little cooler than room temperature. Place all of the Final Dough ingredients in the bowl of a stand mixer with a dough hook attachment and mix on low speed until cleanup stage (see page 31), or 2 to 4 minutes, depending on the mixer. Increase to a medium speed and mix the dough for an additional 30 seconds.

## 3. Fermentation

Take the dough off the mixer and place in a proofing container coated with nonstick cooking spray. The ideal dough temperature is 75°F to 78°F (24°C to 26°C). Cover the dough with plastic and let it rest at room temperature for 2 hours.

After 2 hours at room temperature, loosely shape the dough into a rectangle and place on a parchment-lined half sheet pan. Cover with plastic and refrigerate overnight. Make the butter block (see "Making a Butter Block," page 137) and refrigerate overnight.

3. The mixed dough is placed in a proofing container.

## 4. Stretch and Folds/Degassing

The croissant dough does not go through a traditional stretch-and-fold sequence. Instead it goes through the process of lamination, where the dough receives a series of rolling and folding to build up the layers of dough and butter.

Take the dough out of the refrigerator and place in the freezer for 30 minutes. Take the butter out of the refrigerator and, with it still in the parchment envelope, soften it up by hammering it with the rolling pin until it achieves a pliable consistency. To check pliability, run the slab of butter over the edge of a table or countertop; it should not crack or break, but instead give willingly to the edge. The goal is for the butter and dough to achieve the same consistency before starting the lamination.

Remove the dough from the freezer and roll out to a 16 to 18 x 8-inch (40 to 46 x 20 cm) rectangle. Place the butter block in the centre of the dough, with the short ends of the butter block touching the long edges of the dough. Fold the 2 edges of the dough so that they meet in the centre and press the edges together with your hands.

4a. Centre the butter block on the dough and fold over the edges.

# Making a BUTTER BLOCK

When laminating dough, the finished size of the butter block should equal half the size of the dough rectangle prepared for lamination. European-style butter with a higher (83 percent) fat content works better and is preferred by professional bakers. Regular butter will result in uneven, wavy edges during the hammering, as illustrated in the photo, and needs to be treated specially.*

Fold a piece of 13 x 18-inch (33 x 46 cm) parchment paper in half, crease, and open it up on the table. Place the butter block so the long end of it lines up with the crease. Fold the parchment paper over the butter block and then fold up the remaining three sides of the parchment paper about 2½ inches (6 cm). This creates an envelope around the butter block.

Place the butter on top of a piece of parchment paper. Using a rolling pin, soften the butter by hammering it into a flat rectangle about ³⁄₈ inch (1 cm) thick. The butter should have a soft, plasticlike quality.

Turn the envelope over so that the folded edges are down on the table. Take the rolling pin and roll the butter out toward the edges so that the butter completely fills the envelope. You should now have a perfect butter block that is about 6 x 8 inches (15 x 20 cm) in size.

Using the dough divider, trim the edges of the butter so that they are straight. Use the trimmings to fill in areas that are lacking in butter. The goal is to make a neat rectangle about 5 x 7 inches (13 x 18 cm).

*To use regular unsalted butter: Bring it to room temperature in a stand mixer bowl. Add 0.2 ounces (6 grams/2 teaspoons) flour and mix with a paddle attachment until the butter and flour are completely incorporated. The butter is now ready to spread out on the parchment to make the butter block.

Working on a lightly floured surface and using a rolling pin, roll out the dough lengthwise until it is about ½ inch (1 cm) thick. Using a straightedge or ruler and a pastry wheel, trim the short ends straight. Take one end of the dough and fold it two-thirds of the way over the dough, then fold the remaining third of the dough on top. This is known as a trifold.

4b. Roll out the dough and fold over onto itself in thirds.

On a floured surface, place the dough in front of you with a short end closest to the edge of the table and roll out the dough lengthwise to ½ inch (1 cm) thick. Give another trifold. Place on a sheet pan, cover with plastic, and let rest in freezer for 30 minutes.

After resting, remove the dough from the freezer and give it one final series of rolling and trifolding. Now the dough has had a total of 3 trifolds, which means 27 layers of butter and dough have been created. Not bad!

Place the dough on parchment-lined sheet pan and cover with plastic wrap. Allow the dough to rest for 1 hour in the freezer, then place in the refrigerator until the next day. Before dividing, place the dough in the freezer for an additional 30 to 40 minutes.

## 5. Dividing

Remove the dough from the freezer. Before dividing it into croissant shapes, roll the dough out lengthwise on a floured surface. This time, use the ¼-inch (6 mm) rolling pin guides to create an even thickness throughout the dough (¼-inch [6 mm] wooden dowels can work, too, but they tend to roll). This process can be strenuous, and you may need to let the dough rest for 10 minutes in the freezer between passes. Roll the dough to a width of 11 inches (28 cm) and extend it out to as far as it goes at ¼ inch (6 mm) (approximately 18 inches [46 cm]). If you are not using guides, pay close attention as you roll and maintain an even thickness.

Using the pastry wheel, trim the edges of the dough so they are straight and square.

Measure with a ruler and, with a small cut of the pastry wheel, mark 3-inch (7.5 cm) intervals along the entire length of both long sides of the dough. Use the

5a. Use rolling guides to help maintain the proper thickness.

5b. Measure and mark the dough for cutting.

ruler to line up the corresponding marks from each side and *very lightly* glide the pastry wheel along the edge of the ruler. Do not cut through the dough; simply make a light indentation.

Now, using the ruler again, find the centre of each of these strips and mark them with a small cut along one side only. These marks will be referred to as base marks.

You're almost done! Using the pastry wheel (and ruler if you want to), cut a straight line from each base mark to the corners of the strip opposite it at the top. This will create a series of long triangles.

### 6. Preshaping/Shaping

To shape the croissants, place a triangle of dough in front of you with the tip facing toward you. Starting with the base of the triangle, roll up the dough completely.

### 7. Final Proof

Place the croissants seam side down on a parchment-lined sheet pan. Cover with plastic wrap and let proof at room temperature for 2 to 2½ hours.

Preheat the oven about 30 minutes before baking to 380°F (193°C, gas mark 5), using a convection mode if available at 360°F (182°C, gas mark 4).

### 8. Scoring

The croissants do not need to be scored. Their tension is released between the layers.

### 9. Baking

Just before baking, brush the croissants with egg wash in the direction of the roll, not side to side. (See page 153.)

Bake in the preheated oven for 12 to 15 minutes. The croissants are done when a nice golden brown develops on the crust.

### 10. Cooling/Storage

Remove the croissants from the oven and the sheet pan and place on a wire rack to cool. Enjoy while still warm or at room temperature.

The flaky layers of this dough make the products fairly fragile and unfortunately do not keep for any long periods of time. They are best consumed within a day of baking.

6. Roll up the triangle to form the croissant.

## A TRIANGULAR Shortcut

If the croissants don't need to be in competition form, here's a quicker way to create the long triangles: Mark and cut out 3 x 11-inch (7.5 x 28 cm) strips. Cut each long rectangle once across the diagonal, yielding 2 long triangles. When they are rolled, they are slightly lopsided, but either trim the end so it is straight or just bake them as they are: They will still taste great!

9. Brush the tops of the croissants with egg wash.

## VARIATION: **Pain au Chocolat**

SHAPING AND BAKING: **Medium**

YIELD: **Approximately 18 small units**

FROM THE OUTSIDE, *pain au chocolat* is rather unassuming. Just one bite reveals the simply irresistible surprise of chocolate inside, a perfect afternoon treat paired with coffee or as an after-school snack for children. So go ahead, indulge!

**Prepare Formula Ten (Croissant Dough) through step 5, Dividing** (see pages 134–139), rolling out the final 11-inch (28 cm) wide rectangle. Instead of cutting out triangles as with the croissants, cut straight strips 4½ x 11 inches (11 x 28 cm).

### 6. Preshaping/Shaping

Prepare either the hazelnut filling, chocolate chips, or chocolate batons (see page 154).

Place the chocolate batons or chips just right of the centre line on the dough strip. If using hazelnut filling, use a piping bag to pipe a line of the filling.

Brush the left side of the strip with egg wash (see page 153), then create a log roll by taking the long side of the dough strip and rolling it up and over the line of chocolate and back onto the dough. Gently press to secure the egg-washed seam.

Place the seam side down on the table and with a sharp knife, divide the roll into approximately 2½-inch (6 cm) segments.

6a. Roll the dough around the chocolate or piped filling and seal the ends.

6b. Cut the roll into segments.

**Follow the remaining steps for the croissants, baking at 380°F (193°C, gas mark 5) for 10 to 12 minutes:**

Place seam side down on a parchment-lined sheet pan. Cover with plastic wrap and let proof at room temperature for 2 to 2½ hours.

Preheat the oven about an hour before baking to 380°F (193°C, gas mark 5), using a convection mode if available (see note, page 40). Just before baking, brush the croissants with egg wash in the direction of the roll, not side to side. Bake in the preheated oven for 10 to 12 minutes. The pains are done when a nice golden brown develops on the crust.

Remove the pains from the oven and the sheet pan and place on a wire rack to cool. Enjoy while still warm or at room temperature. After cooling completely, dust with confectioners' sugar if desired.

## Using CHOCOLATE in Baking

Certain chocolates have been made to withstand the heat of baking and still retain much of their integrity. When making *pain au chocolat*, sticks of chocolate called *batons* are the best to use, but usually need to be special ordered. Mini chocolate chips will suffice, especially for the easy-to-please palates of children.

## VARIATION: Hazelnut Snail

SHAPING AND BAKING: **Easy**

YIELD: **12 snails**

HAZELNUTS ARE ONE of the most nutritious nuts, rich not only in flavour, but also in dietary fiber, protein, vitamin E, magnesium, and heart-healthy B vitamins. This tasty delight is delicious and satisfying and pairs perfectly with a morning coffee.

**Prepare Formula Ten (Croissant Dough) through step 5, Dividing** (see pages 134–139), rolling out the dough to approximately 11 x 16 x ¼ inches (28 x 41 x 0.6 mm). Leave the piece whole.

### ADDITIONAL SPECIAL EQUIPMENT
Spatula
5-inch (13-cm) fluted baking form (optional)

6a. Spread the filling out evenly onto the dough.

6b. Roll up the dough and seal the seam.

6c. Cut crosswise through the roll and place snails into forms.

### 6. Preshaping/Shaping

Prepare the hazelnut filling (see page 155). Using a spatula, spread the hazelnut filling onto the surface of the dough, leaving about 1 inch (2.5 cm) bare on one short end. Brush this end with egg wash (see page 153) to help seal the seam after rolling.

Starting from the short end with the filling, roll up the dough like a jelly roll, being careful not to roll too tight. Gently seal the seam.

Using a sharp knife, slice the log every 1 inch (2.5 cm). Take the snails and lay them down into a 5-inch (13 cm) fluted baking form coated with nonstick cooking spray, or place them directly on a parchment-lined sheet pan.

### 7. Final Proof

Place the baking forms on a sheet pan and cover with plastic wrap. Let rest at room temperature until the snails double in size, 1½ to 2 hours.

Preheat the oven about an hour before baking to 380°F (193°C, gas mark 5). If the oven has a convection mode, use it at 360°F (182°C, gas mark 4).

### 8. Scoring

The snails do not need to be scored.

### 9. Baking

Place the sheet pan of hazelnut snails in the oven and bake for 15 to 20 minutes, until golden brown.

### 10. Cooling/Storage

Remove the snails from the sheet pan and cool on a wire rack. Hazelnut snails are best enjoyed within a day of baking and do not freeze well.

## VARIATION: Fruit Danish

SHAPING AND BAKING: **Easy**

YIELD: **8 to 12 pastries**

PAIR CROISSANT DOUGH with fruit and pastry cream for a mouthwatering fruit Danish. It bakes quickly, so use well-drained canned fruit for the topping, such as peaches, apricots, pineapple, and pears. Fresh fruit must be roasted or blanched *al dente*. Firmer fruits, (including apples, nectarines, peaches, pineapples, pears, and plums) work well, but softer fruits, (such as kiwis and berries) do not.

**Prepare Formula Ten (Croissant Dough) through step 5, Dividing** (see pages 134–139, roll out the dough to 8 x 16 x ¼ inches (20 x 41 x 0.6 mm) thick. Using the pastry wheel, divide the dough into 4-inch (10 cm) squares.

### 6. Preshaping/Shaping

Place the 4-inch (10-cm) squares on a parchment-lined sheet pan.

### 7. Final Proof

Cover the squares with plastic wrap and let proof at room temperature for 1½ to 2 hours, checking periodically that there is enough humidity to ensure that the squares do not dry out. The layers should be visible and defined, even though the dough is not fully proofed.

Place the fruit and/or fillings in the centre (see Endless Variations at right) and proof for an additional 15 minutes.

7. Place the fruit in the centre of the square.

### 8. Scoring

The fruit Danish does not need to be scored.

### 9. Baking

Place the sheet pan of fruit Danishes into the oven and bake for 12 to 15 minutes until golden brown.

### 10. Cooling/Storage

Remove from the sheet pan and transfer to a wire rack to cool. If desired, apply a sugar glaze (see Chapter 5, Sweet Embellishments, page 154) to the Danishes while they are still hot. Enjoy the fruit Danishes the day you make them; they taste the best then and do not freeze well.

## ENDLESS VARIATIONS

Spread on a spoonful of pastry cream, chocolate paste, crumb topping, or hazelnut spread and place the fruit on top of it. Or place the fruit down and sprinkle with crumb topping or drizzle with chocolate crackle glaze. Finally, you can simply leave the fruit alone and let its pure flavour stand on its own, always a delicious choice.

# Monkey Bread Deluxe

SHAPING AND BAKING: **Easy**

YIELD: **Varies, depending on the amount of scraps created**

THIS IS MORE of an upscale version of the monkey bread most people are used to, but it could not be any easier to make. It is not overly sweet or sticky and is rather elegant, especially if baked in a fluted tart pan and topped with roasted apples. I make this without fail every time I bake with croissant dough; it is the perfect answer to the question of what to do with all the scrap trimmings just begging to be transformed into something more than remnants.

**Prepare Formula 10 Croissant Dough** (pages 134–139) and save the scrap trimmings during lamination of the dough from the croissants or any of the other variations. Cut them up into pieces the size of a half dollar or smaller. You can even create your own "scraps" if necessary out of new dough.

**ADDITIONAL SPECIAL EQUIPMENT**
Muffin tin or fluted tart pans

## CINNAMON SUGAR

| Ingredient | Metric | Weight | Volume | Baker's % |
|---|---|---|---|---|
| Granulated sugar | 100 g | 3.5 oz | 120 ml | n/a |
| Ground cinnamon | 5 g | 0.17 oz | 2¼ tsp | n/a |

Combine the granulated sugar with the cinnamon and mix together in a bowl.

### 6. Preshaping/Shaping

Toss the dough scraps in the bowl of cinnamon sugar until coated. Place the dough into muffin tins or fluted tart pans coated with nonstick cooking spray. The dough should come about two-thirds of the way up the sides.

**Follow the remaining step of fruit Danish variation:**

Cover with plastic wrap and let proof at room temperature for 1½ to 2 hours, checking the humidity periodically.

*Optional:* Just before baking, top with roasted apple sprinkled with sugar or crumb topping, for a more elaborate creation. Let proof for an additional 15 minutes.

Place in the oven and bake for 12 to 15 minutes, until golden brown. Remove from the sheet pan and transfer to a wire rack to cool.

6a. Cut up the scraps, toss with cinnamon sugar if desired, and place into the baking forms.

## SAVOURY Monkey Bread

You can easily create a savoury version of the monkey bread. Instead of using cinnamon sugar, toss the scraps in finely grated Parmesan cheese. Place in the tins or tart pans and, just before baking, spoon a bit of tomato sauce or your choice of cheese on the top. If you make them in mini-muffin tins, they make great bite-size appetizers.

6b. Top with roasted apples and sugar to add variation and flavour.

# CHAPTER FIVE

# Extras

IN THIS CHAPTER, the "extras" are revealed in two sections: the first showcases recipes using bread as a main ingredient and the second is comprised of additional formulas indispensable for expanding the variety within the breads. There is nothing earth-shatteringly complicated about them. In fact, most are incredibly straightforward and made with just a few select, simple ingredients. Baking bread is fun, but the fruits of the labor are often copious. What happens when your enthusiasm has provided you with enough bread to feed not only your family, but also your neighbors? …and their families? … and their friends? Nothing is more satisfying than sharing warm, homemade bread. But if your freezer is already full and your neighbors are away on vacation, you may not have a choice: You either put your baked goods to use in your own kitchen, or you feed it to the ducks.

I have gathered some basic recipes that include bread as a main ingredient: from bread crumbs and croutons to bread salad and bread pudding. All are easy to make, and some, like the bread pudding, can have both sweet and savoury applications. The second set of formulas will help make your bread creations sing. From sweet to savoury, from glazes to washes, these formulas are merely ideas meant to guide culinary creativity. As you bake and experiment, try different combinations and see what suits your taste buds. Browse cooking magazines and websites and brainstorm your way through your next dinner party or holiday. Check out the latest cookbooks at the bookstore or library. With so many trends and directions in the culinary world, a steady stream of innovation carries chefs into uncharted culinary territory. Be inspired and create!

## BREAD CRUMBS

Bread crumbs are so easy to make, it's a wonder that we buy them at all. All you need is to collect those dried-out slices and ends in an airtight container until you are ready to use them. Bread crumbs can be made out of any combination of breads, but keep in mind that crumbs made from enriched breads such as brioche and challah, will have a shorter shelf life due to their fat content.

Allow the bread to completely dry out. I find that usually after about 2 days of sitting on my kitchen counter, most bread is ready to be "recycled." Cut the bread in half horizontally to expose the inside crumb. Place the bread on a sheet pan and into a 350°F (180°C, gas mark 4) oven for about 20 minutes, or until the crumb is completely dry. Then use either a hand grater or a food processor to grind the bread into the desired size particles. As an option, you can add herbs and spices to introduce a bit of flavour. Store in an airtight container for up to two weeks, or freeze in smaller amounts and then defrost; retoast to remove any moisture as necessary.

## CROUTONS

This is another extremely easy use for older bread. Homemade croutons are delicious and make great toppings for salads, flavourful stuffing bases for meats or vegetables, or tasty garnishes for soups. With a sharp serrated knife, cut the bread into small cubes and place them on a parchment-lined sheet pan. Place into a 370°F (188°C, gas mark 5) oven until they are dry to the touch but don't have too much colour. If the oven has a convection mode, use it at 350°F (180°C, gas mark 4). This time will depend on the type of bread and how dry it already is before being put into the oven.

Remove from the oven and toss in a bowl with a combination of olive oil, salt, ground pepper, and Italian seasoning (or any other dried herbs or spices that you might fancy). This is a bit of a balancing act, as too much oil will make the croutons soggy, but not enough and the seasonings won't stick. Place the croutons back on the parchment-lined sheet pan and into the oven and continue to toast until a golden colour is attained. Remove from oven and let cool completely before use. These can be stored in a plastic food storage bag or other airtight container for up to 1 week.

## BAGEL CHIPS

Everyone loves bagel chips! Whether it's after school or before the game, they have a satisfying crunch and are great plain or for holding lots of your favourite dip. The most dangerous part of making them is cutting the bagels, so take care when slicing them up. Cut thin slices about ⅛ inch (3 mm) thick and lay them on a parchment-lined sheet pan. Place the sheet pan in a 370°F (188°C, gas mark 5) oven and bake until the chips just begin to dry out. If the oven has a convection mode, use it at 350°F (180°C, gas mark 4). Remove the chips and place in a large bowl. Sprinkle the pieces with some olive oil, salt, ground pepper, and garlic powder if desired. Make sure to not use too much oil—it should just coat the surfaces, not end up in the bottom of the bowl. Let them cool and enjoy with your favourite dips or cheeses.

**Alternative:** Bruschetta toasts can be made in the same manner as bagel chips (slice the bread into ¼-inch [0.5 cm] slices).

## BAGUETTE À LA PIZZA

With baguettes, you can make easy appetizers that are substantial enough to serve as a main meal, too. Take a baguette and slice it horizontally down the entire length of the loaf, exposing the crumb structure. With a pastry brush, brush a bit of olive oil on the exposed crumb (the savoury mixture on page 157 works great here!). Put the baguette on a parchment-lined sheet pan and place in a 360°F (182°C, gas mark 4) preheated oven for 4 to 5 minutes, just enough to warm the bread but not enough to brown it. Remove it from the oven and add any desired toppings, such as salsa, pizza sauce, roasted peppers, fresh tomatoes, or grated cheese. Place back in the oven and bake until the cheese melts or the toppings are hot. Remove, cut into desired sizes, and serve warm.

**Variation:** You can make great garlic bread this way to serve with dinner by brushing on a savoury mixture of olive oil, melted butter, crushed garlic, salt, pepper, and Italian seasonings.

## BREAD SALAD

Bread salad is an excellent way to use up stale baguettes or similar bread. Many of the ingredients are staples in the kitchen, so preparation is a breeze, and it is particularly flavourful in the summer when tomatoes are local and fresh. If you don't have any stale bread on hand, it is easy to dry out in the oven. First cut the bread into ½-inch to 1-inch (1 to 2.5 cm) cubes or, for a more rustic look, tear the pieces into comparable sizes. Then place the pieces on a parchment-lined sheet pan and put into the preheated 350°F (180°C, gas mark 4) oven for 5 to 10 minutes, depending on the freshness of the bread. As the bread cools, cut up 3 medium tomatoes, 1 medium red onion, and ¼ cup (25 g) of pitted kalamata olives in bite-size pieces. Place tomatoes, onion, and olives into a bowl and mix together with ¼ cup (60 ml) of olive oil, ¼ cup (60 ml) of balsamic vinegar, 1 teaspoon (3 g) of minced garlic, salt, and fresh ground pepper. Toss the bread cubes in the mixture and let sit for 20 to 30 minutes, allowing the bread to soften and absorb the juices. Serve and enjoy!

## FRENCH TOAST

I love to make French toast with challah or a brioche loaf, but any homemade bread will be delicious. For best results, cut the bread into generous ¾-inch (2 cm) slices about an hour before using. This allows you to soak the bread longer without the pieces falling apart, giving a fuller flavour and texture to the French toast.

Whisk all ingredients together and let stand for 5 minutes to let the flavourings infuse. Pour the mixture into a deep-dish plate with enough room to soak the bread, preferably 2 or 3 slices at a time. Lay each side in the mixture, allowing the liquid to soak halfway into the bread. Turn the slices over and let soak on the other side. You can place the dipped pieces on a cooling rack to "drip dry" for a couple of minutes. In a large skillet on medium heat, melt enough butter to just cover the bottom of the pan. When ready, place the dipped slices in the skillet and cook on both sides until the desired colour is achieved. As you cook the French toast, you will occasionally need to add more butter to

| Ingredient | Metric | Weight | Volume |
| --- | --- | --- | --- |
| Whole eggs | 150 g | 5.2 oz | 3 eggs |
| Milk | 500 g | 1 lb, 1.6 oz | 530 ml |
| Vanilla extract | 20 g | 0.7 oz | 20 ml |
| Granulated sugar | 35 g | 1.2 oz | 3 tsp |
| Ground cinnamon | ½ g | 0.01 oz | ¼ tsp |
| Salt | Pinch | Pinch | Pinch |

the skillet. Serve the traditional way, sprinkled with confectioners' sugar and topped with maple syrup, or try making a sandwich by using jam or fresh fruit in the centre.

## BREAD PUDDING

Bread pudding has a long history, dating back to the eleventh century, when frugal cooks of the times did the same thing that we do today: investigate different ways to use up stale bread. Once known as the "poor man's pudding," bread pudding is no longer defined by its humble roots and today graces the menus of many upscale restaurants. The beauty behind this layered, custard-baked delight is in its variety, with the ingredients and the flavourings being as flexible as the creator. Here are two variations for you to try, one sweet and one savoury.

### Sweet Bread Pudding

| Ingredient | Metric | Weight | Volume |
|---|---|---|---|
| Milk | 453 g | 1 lb | 475 ml |
| Heavy cream | 113 g | 4 oz | 120 ml |
| Granulated sugar | 50 g | 1.7 oz | |
| Salt | 2 g | 0.07 oz | ½ tsp |
| Whole eggs | 226 g | 7.9 oz | 5 eggs |
| Vanilla extract or orange blossom water | 15 or 25 g | 0.5 or 0.8 oz | 15 or 25 ml |
| Stale bread, cubed into ¾-inch (2 cm) pieces | 250 g | 8.8 oz | |
| Aniseed (optional) | ½ g | 0.01 oz | ½ tsp |
| Candied orange peel (optional) | 75 g | 2.6 oz | |

In a large saucepan, combine the milk, heavy cream, sugar, and salt, and bring to a boil over medium-high heat. In a separate bowl, whisk together the eggs and the vanilla extract or orange blossom water until pale yellow. Temper the eggs with some of the hot milk mixture and then return the eggs back to the main milk mixture, stirring constantly. (See Basic Egg Tempering, page 154.) Strain the custard if necessary.

Brush the inside of an 8-inch (20 cm) round casserole dish with melted butter. Fill the casserole dish to the top with the bread cubes and optionally toss with the aniseeds and orange peel. Slowly pour the warm milk and egg mixture over the bread cubes.

## Baking in a WATER BATH

A water bath is used to bake many delicate foods and egg-based desserts, insulating them from direct oven heat and allowing slow cooking. Pull the middle oven rack out and place the water bath pan in the centre. Fill it with about 1 inch (2.5 cm) of very hot tap water and place the baking dish in the centre. Carefully pour in more hot water until the level is three-quarters up the side of the baking dish. Carefully slide the oven rack back into the oven and bake as recommended.

The bread pudding is baked in a water bath (see Baking in a Water Bath, page 151) at 350°F (180°C, gas mark 4) for 1 hour, or until the egg mixture is completely set.

## SAVOURY BREAD PUDDING

In a large saucepan, combine the milk, heavy cream, and salt and bring to a boil over medium-high heat. In a separate bowl, whisk together the eggs with the black pepper, Italian seasoning, and garlic until pale yellow. Temper the eggs with some of the hot milk mixture and then return the eggs back to the main milk mixture, stirring constantly. Strain the custard if necessary.

In a medium skillet on medium-high heat, melt the butter and sauté the red and yellow bell peppers and onions until tender; remove from heat and set aside. Brush the inside of an 8-inch (2 cm) round casserole dish with melted butter. In a bowl, toss the bread cubes with the sautéed vegetables and half of the grated cheese. Fill the casserole dish to the top with the bread mixture and top with the remaining cheese. Slowly pour the warm milk and egg mixture over the bread cubes. The bread pudding is baked in a water bath at 350°F (180°C, gas mark 4) for 1 hour, or until the egg mixture is completely set.

| Ingredient | Metric | Weight | Volume |
| --- | --- | --- | --- |
| Milk | 453 g | 1 lb | 475 ml |
| Heavy cream | 113 g | 4 oz | 120 ml |
| Salt | 50 g | 1.7 oz | 1½ tsp |
| Whole eggs | 226 | 7.9 oz | 5 eggs |
| Ground black pepper | 1 g | 0.03 oz | ½ tsp |
| Italian seasoning | ½ g | 0.01 oz | ½ tsp |
| Fresh minced garlic | 1 clove | 1 clove | 1 clove |
| Fresh red bell pepper, medium | 1 | 1 | 1 |
| Fresh yellow bell pepper, medium | 1 | 1 | 1 |
| Onions, medium | ½ each | ½ each | ½ each |
| Unsalted butter | 28 g | 1 oz | |
| Grated Gruyère cheese | 150 g | 5.2 oz | |
| Stale bread, cubed into ¾-inch (2 cm) pieces | 250 g | 8.8 oz | |

# Washes and Glazes

## EGG WASH

| Ingredient | Metric | Weight | Volume |
|---|---|---|---|
| Whole egg | 100 g | 3.5 oz | 2 eggs |
| Egg yolk | 25 g | 0.8 oz | 1 yolk |
| Water | 2 g | 0.06 oz | 5 ml |
| Salt | Pinch | Pinch | Pinch |

By hand or machine, whisk all of the ingredients together in a bowl until completely smooth. Let stand for about 30 minutes before use. Apply with a soft bristled brush.

## SUGAR GLAZE

| Ingredient | Metric | Weight | Volume |
|---|---|---|---|
| Confectioners' sugar | 150 g | 5.2 oz | |
| Corn syrup | 9 g | 0.3 oz | 15 ml |
| Milk | 33 g | 1.1 oz | 30 ml |
| Vanilla extract | 2 g | 0.07 oz | 2 ml |

In a saucepan, warm corn syrup, milk, and vanilla extract to 140°F (60°C). Combine the powdered sugar into the milk mixture, stirring constantly until a smooth consistency is achieved. The glaze can be used immediately, or cover with plastic wrap touching the surface and refrigerate overnight.

## CHOCOLATE GLAZE

| Ingredient | Metric | Weight | Volume |
|---|---|---|---|
| Granulated sugar | 167 g | 5.8 oz | |
| Almond flour | 80 g | 2.8 oz | |
| Vegetable oil | 12 g | 0.4 oz | 10 ml |
| Corn flour (masa harina) | 6 g | 0.2 oz | 1 tbsp |
| Cocoa powder | 6 g | 0.2 oz | 1 tbsp |
| Vanilla extract | 17 g | 0.6 oz | 18 ml |
| Egg whites | 80 g | 2.8 oz | 2 egg whites |

*Note: Be sure to use almond flour and not ground almonds for this recipe.*

Place all of the above ingredients in a stainless-steel bowl and stir together till a smooth consistency is achieved. When applied to the top of a brioche with a pastry bag, the glaze should run a bit, but not completely, off the side of the product. The consistency can be adjusted by either holding back some or adding a bit more of the egg whites. After glazing, optional toppings include pearl sugar, chopped almond slivers, or a heavy dusting of confectioners' sugar for a cracking effect.

# Sweet Embellishments

### HAZELNUT FILLING

| Ingredient | Metric | Weight | Volume |
|---|---|---|---|
| Hazelnut or almond flour | 125 g | 4.4 oz | |
| Granulated sugar | 100 g | 3.5 oz | |
| Light corn syrup | 25 g | 0.8 oz | 24 ml |
| Water | 62 g | 2.1 oz | 90 ml |
| Ground cinnamon | 1 g | 0.03 oz | ¼ tsp |

Combine nut flour, sugar, corn syrup, cinnamon, and half of the water in a bowl. Blend together by hand with a spatula or mixing spoon, slowly adding the remaining water until a smooth consistency is achieved that will not tear the dough when spread on. More water can be added if necessary, and the consistency can still be adjusted with water on the following day. Store for up to 5 days in the refrigerator.

### LEMON CURD

| Ingredient | Metric | Weight | Volume |
|---|---|---|---|
| Egg yolks | 120 g | 4.2 oz | 5 yolks |
| Granulated sugar | 100 g | 3.5 oz | |
| Fresh lemon juice | 100 g | 3.5 oz | 120 ml |
| Lemon zest | of ½ lemon | of ½ lemon | of ½ lemon |
| Unsalted butter | 55 g | 1.9 oz | |

Put all ingredients in a stainless-steel pot and cook over medium heat, stirring continuously, until the mixture becomes thick. Make sure not to burn the bottom of the pot. Strain if needed, and chill.

## Basic EGG TEMPERING

Tempering is a method for blending uncooked eggs into a hot liquid or sauce without scrambling them. Prepare the hot milk and the egg mixture in the formula and follow these steps to slowly raise the temperature of the egg mixture to ensure successful incorporation with the hot milk mixture:

Add a small, steady stream of hot milk mixture into the eggs, simultaneously whisking the two together. This gradually raises the temperature of the egg and slightly cools the milk.

Continue to do this until the egg mixture warms up as close as possible to the milk mixture. At this point, return the warmed egg mixture back into the hot milk mixture, still whisking constantly.

The egg mixture should incorporate smoothly. Small lumps can be removed by straining the mixture through a sieve or cheesecloth, but you will need to start over with new ingredients if they coagulate more than that.

## PASTRY CREAM

| Ingredient | Metric | Weight | Volume |
|---|---|---|---|
| Vanilla bean (optional) | ⅓ of bean | ⅓ of bean | ⅓ of bean |
| Whole milk | 333 g | 11.7 oz | 315 ml |
| 1st Granulated sugar | 42 g | 1.4 oz | 3 tbsp |
| Egg yolks | 62 g | 2.1 oz | 2 yolks |
| Cornstarch | 25 g | 0.8 oz | 2½ tbsp |
| 2nd Granulated sugar | 42 g | 1.4 oz | 3 tbsp |
| Unsalted butter | 22 g | 0.7 | |
| Vanilla extract | 5 g | 0.1 oz | 5 ml |

Split the vanilla bean in half, if using. In a saucepan, bring the milk, split vanilla bean, and first portion of sugar to a boil. While waiting for the milk mixture to boil, whisk the egg yolks together in a separate bowl, until light yellow. Combine the second portion of sugar with the cornstarch and whisk into yolk mixture until smooth. Let the milk mixture cool off just a bit and then temper the egg mixture with it (see Basic Egg Tempering, page 154). Pour the tempered egg mixture into the remaining milk mixture and return to a boil, stirring constantly. When the mixture thickens, remove from the heat and stir in the butter and vanilla extract. Cover immediately so that the plastic wrap is touching the surface of the cream and place in the refrigerator to cool. Use within 2 days of preparation.

## ROASTED APPLES *OR* APPLE FILLING

| Ingredient | Metric | Weight | Volume |
|---|---|---|---|
| Large, firm apples (Granny Smith) | 2 each | 2 each | 2 each |
| Unsalted butter | 22 g | 0.7 oz | |
| Brown sugar | 22 g | 0.7 oz | 2 tbsp |
| Vanilla bean, split | ½ each | ½ each | ½ each |
| Cornstarch (optional) | 5 g | 0.1 oz | 1 tsp |
| Ground cinnamon | Pinch | Pinch | Pinch |

*For roasting:* Peel and remove the core from the apples, then cut into medium slices. Melt the butter in a large skillet, then add the sugar and split vanilla bean. Place the fruit in the pan and quickly simmer, carefully browning the fruit evenly. Remove from the heat when a semisoft texture is achieved. Remove the vanilla bean before using.

*For filling:* Peel and remove the core from the apples, then cut into cubes. Mix together the cornstarch, sugar, and cinnamon. Toss the apple cubes in the sugar mixture. Melt the butter in a large skillet and add the split vanilla bean. Place the fruit in the pan and simmer, carefully browning the fruit evenly. Remove from the heat when a semisoft texture is achieved. Remove the vanilla bean before using.

*Almost any firm fruit, such as peaches, plums, nectarines, and cherries, can be substituted for the apples.*

## TRADITIONAL CRUMB TOPPING

| Ingredient | Metric | Weight | Volume |
|---|---|---|---|
| Bread flour | 126 g | 4.4 oz | |
| Light brown sugar | 97 g | 3.4 oz | |
| Ground cinnamon | Pinch | Pinch | Pinch |
| Salt | Pinch | Pinch | Pinch |
| Butter, cold, cubed | 92 g | 3.2 oz | |

Combine all of the above ingredients in a bowl and rub together with hands until the mixture resembles a nicely textured crumb topping. This can also be made in a 5-quart (5 L) mixer with the paddle attachment or a food processor, but be careful not to overmix. Use immediately, chill in the refrigerator for a couple of days, or freeze for up to 1 month.

## SPECIAL NUT CRUMB TOPPING

| Ingredient | Metric | Weight | Volume |
|---|---|---|---|
| Pecans, toasted | 45 g | 1.5 oz | |
| Whole rolled oats | 45 g | 1.5 oz | |
| Sugar | 60 g | 2.1 oz | |
| Bread flour | 76 g | 2.6 oz | |
| Orange zest | ¾ of orange | ¾ of orange | ¾ of orange |
| Cinnamon | 2 g | 0.07 oz | 1 tsp |
| Salt | .33 g | 0.01 oz | Pinch |
| Baking powder | .33 g | 0.01 oz | Pinch |
| Unsalted butter, melted | 66 g | 2.3 oz | |

Chop the toasted pecans and oats in a food processor to a medium texture. Combine all of the dry ingredients in a bowl. Add the melted butter and rub together with hands. Use immediately, chill in the refrigerator for a couple of days, or freeze for up to 1 month.

## CINNAMON SPICE MIX

| Ingredient | Metric | Weight | Volume |
|---|---|---|---|
| Granulated sugar | 100 g | 3.5 oz | |
| Ground cinnamon | 5 g | 0.17 oz | 2 ¼ tsp |
| Ground cardamom (optional) | 1 g | 0.03 oz | ¼ tsp |
| Ground cloves (optional) | 1 g | 0.03 oz | ¼ tsp |

# Savoury Inspirations

## SAVOURY OIL

| Ingredient | Metric | Weight | Volume |
| --- | --- | --- | --- |
| Olive oil | 215 g | 7.5 oz | 240 ml |
| Minced garlic | 16 g | 0.5 oz | |
| Fresh rosemary, chopped | 1 g | 0.03 oz | |
| Salt | 3 g | 0.1 oz | |
| Pepper | ½ g | 0.01 oz | |
| Oregano, dried | 1 g | 0.03 oz | |

Combine all of the ingredients in a bowl. For best flavour, let the infusion stand at room temperature for 12 to 24 hours before using.

## CARAMELIZED ONIONS

| Ingredient | Metric | Weight | Volume |
| --- | --- | --- | --- |
| Sweet onions, large | 3 whole large | 3 whole large | 3 whole large |
| Unsalted butter | 60 g | 2.1 oz | |
| Olive oil | 10 g | 0.3 oz | 45 ml |
| Balsamic vinegar | 20 g | 2 oz | 60 ml |
| Salt | 2 g | 0.07 oz | |
| Light brown sugar | 25 g | 0.8 oz | |

Peel and cut the onions into julienne-size pieces. Melt the butter and oil in a large skillet. Add the onions and toss immediately to coat with butter mixture. Add the vinegar, salt, and brown sugar, and stir until salt and sugar are completely dissolved. Cook at a slow simmer until the onions are glassy and translucent. Drain off the excess liquid and allow to cool.

## ONION FILLING

| Ingredient | Metric | Weight | Volume |
| --- | --- | --- | --- |
| Onions, large | 1 | 1 | 1 |
| Olive oil | 15 g | 0.53 oz | 15 ml |
| Bread flour | 3 g | 0.1 oz | |
| Salt | 3 g | 0.1 oz | |

To prepare the filling, peel and finely dice the onion and sprinkle on the salt. Heat the oil in a small skillet, add the salted onion, and sauté for about a minute. Sprinkle the flour over the diced onions and sauté until they attain a medium/soft consistency and are coated with a milky paste. Remove from the heat and set aside to cool a bit.

## BASIL PESTO

| Ingredient | Metric | Weight | Volume |
|---|---|---|---|
| Fresh basil, shredded | 230 g | 8.1 oz | |
| Fresh garlic cloves | 10 | 10 | 10 |
| Freshly ground pepper | 3 g | 0.1 oz | 1 tsp |
| Salt | 4 g | 0.14 oz | ½ tsp |
| Extra-virgin olive oil | 60–90 g | 2.1–3.1 oz | 62–92 ml |
| Grated Parmesan cheese | 80 g | 2.8 oz | |
| Toasted pine nuts (optional) | 80 g | 2.8 oz | |

Wash and coarsely chop the basil with a knife. In a food processor, pulse together the basil, garlic, pepper, and salt. Slowly add ⅓ cup (60 g) olive oil to make a smooth paste. Add the cheese and pulse, adjusting the consistency with more olive oil, if necessary. Carefully pulse the pine nuts, if using, into the pesto, retaining some medium texture with the nuts. Store the pesto in refrigerator in an airtight container for up to 1 week.

## BASIL PESTO SPREAD

| Ingredients | Metric | Weight | Volume |
|---|---|---|---|
| Basil pesto | 140 g | 4.9 oz | |
| Boursin cheese | 150 g | 5.2 oz | 1 package (5.2 oz) |

Combine the pesto and Boursin cheese in a bowl and mix until smooth, adjusting the consistency if necessary by adding a little milk.

## BOURSIN SPREAD

| Ingredient | Metric | Weight | Volume |
|---|---|---|---|
| Milk | 24 g | 0.8 oz | 24 ml |
| Boursin cheese | 150 g | 5.2 oz | 1 package (5.2 oz) |

Combine the milk and Boursin cheese in a bowl and mix until smooth, adjusting the consistency if necessary by adding a little milk. When spooned, the spread should retain its shape without running.

## PIZZA SAUCES

### Basic Red Sauce

| Ingredient | Metric | Weight | Volume |
|---|---|---|---|
| Olive oil | 10 g | 0.3 oz | 15 ml |
| Onion, chopped | 145 g | 5 oz | |
| White or red wine | 50 g | 1.7 oz | 75 ml |
| Diced tomatoes | 790 g | 28-oz can | |
| Crushed tomatoes | 1580 g | Two 28-oz cans | |
| Tomato puree | 55 g | 1.9 oz | 4 tbsp |
| Sugar | 20 g | 0.7 oz | 2 tbsp |
| Ground pepper | 1 g | 0.03 oz | 1/2 tsp |
| Fresh minced garlic | 16 g | 0.56 oz | 1½ tbsp |
| Fresh rosemary, chopped | 1 g | 0.03 oz | 1 tsp |
| Oregano, dried | 1 g | 0.03 oz | ½ tsp |
| Salt | 7 g | 0.2 oz | 240 ml |

### Cream Sauce

| Ingredient | Metric | Weight | Volume |
|---|---|---|---|
| Basic red sauce | ½ of batch | ½ of batch | ½ of batch |
| Heavy cream | 230 g | 8 oz | ½ pt |

To make the basic red sauce, heat a large sauté pan with the olive oil and add the chopped onions. Sauté for 2 minutes and then deglaze by adding the wine. Continue to cook the onions until they are clear. Add all of the remaining ingredients and bring to a boil. Reduce the heat and cook at a low simmer for 1 hour. Remove about half (4 cups [1 kg]) of the sauce, and set aside to cool.

To make the cream sauce variation, add the cream to the remaining sauce in the pan and bring to a boil. Remove from the heat and set aside to cool.

Both sauces keep in the refrigerator for about 3 days or can be frozen for up to 1 month.

# Troubleshooting

Every baker dreams of a perfect bake, the one in which everything comes together just right. When the synergy happens, it is pure magic. But professional bakers constantly struggle to keep all the variables in balance just as much as the home baker—it's just that they usually have much more experience in identifying the problems as they occur and are able to make corrections before it is too late.

Troubleshooting is part of this process. The following section will help identify some of the typical problems associated with bread baking and teach the adjustments.

## PROBLEMS WITH PRE-FERMENTS AND MIXING

A poolish in three stages (from left to right): underdeveloped, perfectly developed, and overdeveloped

A biga in three stages (from left to right): underdeveloped, perfectly developed, and overdeveloped. (Note: The sponge used in this book will look similar.)

Three doughs (from left to right): no salt in the dough—pulls like taffy; nicely mixed; and overmixed—shiny and gummy

## PROBLEMS WITH SHAPING AND BAKING

The rolls on the right have been shaped nicely.

The rolls on the left have been overshaped.

Three scored baguettes (from left to right): Incorrect, correct, incorrect

From left to right: overbaked (too dark), nicely baked (good colour), underbaked (too light)

These three baguettes started with the same weight and shape (from left to right):

**Underproofed**—dough did not achieve potential volume during baking

**Nicely proofed**—dough expanded during baking and lifted nicely at the cuts

**Overproofed**—dough "expired" and the final shape lacks lift and definition

Cross sections of the same three baguettes (from left to right):

**Underproofed**—notice the round profile and tighter crumb structure

**Nicely proofed**—a softer, more relaxed profile and nice open crumb structure

**Overproofed**—an oval profile with a long, flat bottom

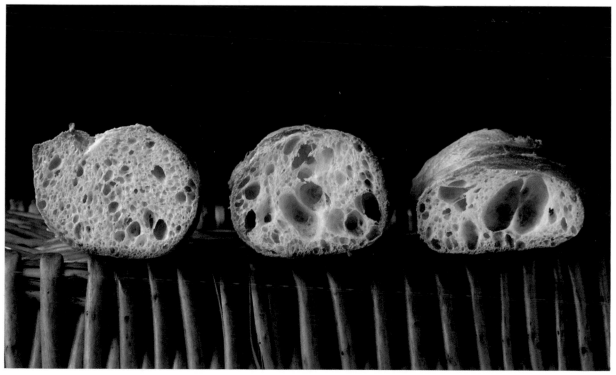

Can you spot the ideal baguette? (from left to right):

**No steam**—the crust is dull without any shine

**Shaped with seam up**—the seam is visible running through the centre of the baguette

**Uneven cuts**—the baguette is mis-shapen through uneven cuts

**Ideal**—no obvious mistakes or glaring imperfections

**Overproofed**—baguette allowed to proof too long, resulting in little lift and definition.

| If : | Then: |
| --- | --- |
| dough tears during shaping | dough is underdeveloped |
| bread "blows out" on the sides | scoring cuts are not deep enough *or* seam-side is on top of the bread |
| bread looks misshapen | scoring cuts are irregular |
| crust is dull | little or no steam during baking |
| dough feels tacky | salt omitted from the formula |
| lack of browning | pre-ferment was overfermented or bread was overproofed |

# Charts and Conversions

## METRIC & U.S. STANDARD WEIGHTS

| | | |
|---|---|---|
| 1 gram | = | 0.035 ounces |
| 1 ounce | = | 28.35 grams |
| 1 pound | = | 453.6 grams |
| 1 kilogram | = | 35.27 ounces |

## ARITHMETIC CONVERSIONS

| To Convert | into | Multiply by |
|---|---|---|
| Grams | Ounces | 0.035 |
| Ounces | Grams | 28.35 |

## TEMPERATURE CONVERSIONS

| | | | | | | | |
|---|---|---|---|---|---|---|---|
| Degrees in Celsius | x | 1.8 | + | 32 | = | Degrees in Fahrenheit |
| Degrees in Fahrenheit | – | 32 | x | 0.555 | = | Degrees in Celsius |

## YEAST CONVERSIONS

The formulas in this book were created with instant yeast. To convert the instant yeast amounts to either fresh yeast or active dry yeast, use the following conversion equations:

| | | | | |
|---|---|---|---|---|
| Grams (or ounces) of instant yeast | X | 2.5 | = | Grams (or ounces) of fresh (cake) yeast |
| Grams (or ounces) of instant yeast | X | 1.25 | = | Grams (or ounces) of active dry yeast |

These conversions differ slightly from the manufacturers' recommended amounts. The bread doughs in this book come off the mixer at slightly cooler temperatures, and the general rule of thumb among bakers is to use just a bit more instant yeast than recommended.

Keep in mind that active dry yeast will need to be dissolved in warm water (100°F [38°C]) before being added to the dough. The change in temperature will cause the dough to ferment at a faster rate, so either be mindful during the fermentation stages or allow the water to cool down to the temperature specified in the formulas.

## BAKER'S PERCENTAGE

Professional bakers express many of their formulas in baker's percentage because it allows different formulas to be easily compared. Many serious home bakers have adopted this approach as well, because it allows a formula to be more easily increased or decreased as the desired yield requires. However, acclimation takes some time; it is not like the percentages taught in math class. Each ingredient in the formula is expressed as a percentage of the total amount of flour in the formula (flour being the predominant ingredient). Therefore flour's percentage is constant at 100 percent. If there is more than one type of flour listed, then the combination of the weights of all flours would be 100 percent.

For example, in the following hypothetical formula, the bread flour and whole wheat flour percentages add up to 100 percent.

| | | | |
|---|---|---|---|
| Bread flour: | 800 g | = | 80% |
| Whole wheat flour: | 200 g | = | 20% |
| Water: | 650 g | = | 65% |
| Salt: | 30 g | = | 3% |
| Yeast: | 20 g | = | 2% |

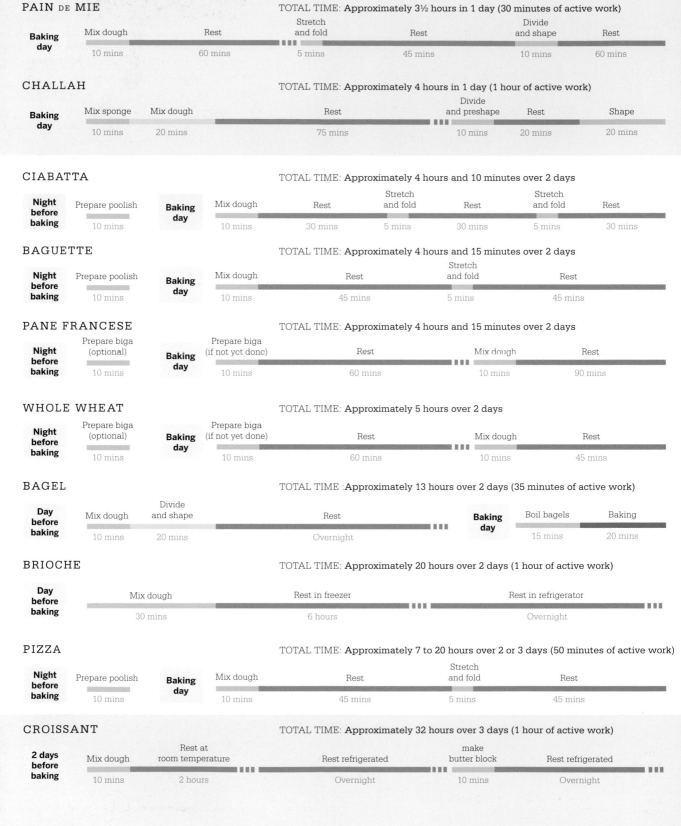

## 1 DAY

### PAIN DE MIE
TOTAL TIME: Approximately 3½ hours in 1 day (30 minutes of active work)

**Baking day**

| Mix dough | Rest | Stretch and fold | Rest | Divide and shape | Rest |
|---|---|---|---|---|---|
| 10 mins | 60 mins | 5 mins | 45 mins | 10 mins | 60 mins |

### CHALLAH
TOTAL TIME: Approximately 4 hours in 1 day (1 hour of active work)

**Baking day**

| Mix sponge | Mix dough | Rest | Divide and preshape | Rest | Shape |
|---|---|---|---|---|---|
| 10 mins | 20 mins | 75 mins | 10 mins | 20 mins | 20 mins |

## 2 DAYS

### CIABATTA
TOTAL TIME: Approximately 4 hours and 10 minutes over 2 days

**Night before baking** — Prepare poolish — 10 mins

**Baking day**

| Mix dough | Rest | Stretch and fold | Rest | Stretch and fold | Rest |
|---|---|---|---|---|---|
| 10 mins | 30 mins | 5 mins | 30 mins | 5 mins | 30 mins |

### BAGUETTE
TOTAL TIME: Approximately 4 hours and 15 minutes over 2 days

**Night before baking** — Prepare poolish — 10 mins

**Baking day**

| Mix dough | Rest | Stretch and fold | Rest |
|---|---|---|---|
| 10 mins | 45 mins | 5 mins | 45 mins |

### PANE FRANCESE
TOTAL TIME: Approximately 4 hours and 15 minutes over 2 days

**Night before baking** — Prepare biga (optional) — 10 mins

**Baking day**

| Prepare biga (if not yet done) | Rest | Mix dough | Rest |
|---|---|---|---|
| 10 mins | 60 mins | 10 mins | 90 mins |

### WHOLE WHEAT
TOTAL TIME: Approximately 5 hours over 2 days

**Night before baking** — Prepare biga (optional) — 10 mins

**Baking day**

| Prepare biga (if not yet done) | Rest | Mix dough | Rest |
|---|---|---|---|
| 10 mins | 60 mins | 10 mins | 45 mins |

### BAGEL
TOTAL TIME: Approximately 13 hours over 2 days (35 minutes of active work)

**Day before baking**

| Mix dough | Divide and shape | Rest |
|---|---|---|
| 10 mins | 20 mins | Overnight |

**Baking day**

| Boil bagels | Baking |
|---|---|
| 15 mins | 20 mins |

### BRIOCHE
TOTAL TIME: Approximately 20 hours over 2 days (1 hour of active work)

**Day before baking**

| Mix dough | Rest in freezer | Rest in refrigerator |
|---|---|---|
| 30 mins | 6 hours | Overnight |

### PIZZA
TOTAL TIME: Approximately 7 to 20 hours over 2 or 3 days (50 minutes of active work)

**Night before baking** — Prepare poolish — 10 mins

**Baking day**

| Mix dough | Rest | Stretch and fold | Rest |
|---|---|---|---|
| 10 mins | 45 mins | 5 mins | 45 mins |

## 3 DAYS

### CROISSANT
TOTAL TIME: Approximately 32 hours over 3 days (1 hour of active work)

**2 days before baking**

| Mix dough | Rest at room temperature | Rest refrigerated | make butter block | Rest refrigerated |
|---|---|---|---|---|
| 10 mins | 2 hours | Overnight | 10 mins | Overnight |

Baking
45 mins

Rest
60 mins

Baking
30 mins

This chart illustrates the time required for each of the bread formulas and is intended to be a helpful tool for planning your baking. The ten formulas are sorted into three groups based on the number of days involved in preparation (one, two, and three). For ease of comparison, the timelines are to scale within each group. The baking time is sorted into active work involved (yellow), the resting periods (brown), and baking times (gray). *Note: These general timelines should not replace the instructions given in the actual formulas.*

| Divide | Rest | Baking |
|---|---|---|
| 5 mins | 30 mins | 40 mins |

| Divide and preshape | Rest | Final shape | Rest | Baking |
|---|---|---|---|---|
| 5 mins | 30 mins | 10 mins | 60 mins | 30 mins |

| | Dividing | Rest | Baking |
|---|---|---|---|
| | 5 mins | 45 mins | 20 mins |

| Stretch and fold | Rest | Mix Dough | Rest | Baking |
|---|---|---|---|---|
| 5 mins | 45 mins | 10 mins | 60 mins | 45 mins |

| **Baking day** | Rest at room temperature | Divide and shape | Rest | Baking |
|---|---|---|---|---|
| | 30 mins | 20 mins | 60 mins | 30 mins |

| Divide and preshape | Rest | Shape and top | Baking |
|---|---|---|---|
| 10 mins | 4-18 hours | 15 mins | 15 mins |

| **Day before baking** | Rest in freezer | 2 trifolds | Rest in freezer | 1 trifold | Rest in freezer | Rest refrigerated |
|---|---|---|---|---|---|---|
| | 30 mins | 20 mins | 30 mins | 10 mins | 60 mins | overnight |

| **Baking day** | Rest in freezer | Divide and shape | Rest at room temperature | Baking |
|---|---|---|---|---|
| | 30 mins | 20 mins | 2 hours | 20 mins |

# Ingredients, Tools, and Equipment

**Artisan Food**
Broadgate House
Grasmere
LA22 9TA
England
www.artisan-food.com
*A comprehensive source of information on the organic food community in the UK*

**Bakemark**
Skerton Road
Old Trafford
Manchester
M16 ONJ
England
www.bakemark.co.uk
*A comprehensive source of baking ingredients*

**Hobbs House Bakery**
Unit 6, Chipping Edge Industrial Estate
Hatters Lane
Chipping Sodbury, Bristol
BS37 6AA
England
www.hobbshousebakery.co.uk
*Great resource for handmade bread bakers*

**Kitchenware**
Unit 5A
Avon gorge Ind Est
Portview Road
Avonmouth, Bristol
BS11 9LQ
www.kitchenware.co.uk
*A complete source of kitchenware and baking equipment*

**The Recipes Shop**
www.free-recipes.co.uk
*An excellent resource for culinary tips and baking supplies*

**Little Salkeld Watermill**
The Watermill, Little Salkeld
Penrith, Cumbria
CA1O 1NN
England
www.organicmill.co.uk
*Millers of organic flours*

**A unique source for books on baking, organic stoneground flour and other ingredientsKing Arthur Flour**
135 Route 5 South
Norwich, VT 05055 USA
www.kingarthurflour.com
*A premier baking resource for flour, baking ingredients, tools, and education*

**Bob's Red Mill Natural Foods**
13521 SE Pheasant Court
Milwaukie, OR 97222 USA
www.bobsredmill.com
*A leading resource in stone milling and a wide diversity of whole grains*

**Penzeys Spices**
19300 West Janacek Court
Brookfield, WI USA
www.penzeys.com
*A comprehensive offering of spices, seasonings, and herbs*

**Breadhitz**
www.breadhitz.com
*Tutorial DVDs on baking handmade and decorative breads; tools*

**JB Prince**
36 East 31st Street
New York, NY 10016 USA
www.jbprince.com
*A great resource for culinary tools and equipment*

**Right On Scales**
P.O. Box 710374
Santee, CA 92072-0374 USA
www.rightonscales.com
*A comprehensive resource for digital scales*

**Fantes**
1006 South Ninth Street
Philadelphia, PA 19147-4798 USA
www.fantes.com
*An extremely complete source
of kitchenware*

**Bridge Kitchenware**
711 3rd Avenue
New York, NY 10017 USA
www.bridgekitchenware.com
*Professional-grade bakeware and tools*

**TMB Baking**
480 Grandview Drive
South San Francisco, CA 94080 USA
www.tmbbaking.com
*Good source for couche material, baskets,
and hand tools*

**Maine Wood Heat**
254 Fr. Rasle Road
Norridgewock, ME 04957 USA
www.mainewoodheat.com
*North American distributor of Le Panyol
wood-fired oven cores*

**C.H.I.P.S.**
10777 Mazoch Road
Weimar, TX 78962 USA
www.chipsbooks.com
*Great selection of books on baking, baking
technology, and other culinary fields*

# Recommended Reading

*The Complete Bread Machine* by Marjie Lambert
(Apple Press, UK, 2003)

*Artisan Baking Across America* by Maggie Glezer
(New York: Artisan, 2000)

*The Best Bread Ever* by Charles Van Over (New York:
Broadway Books, 1997)

*A Blessing of Bread* by Maggie Glezer (New York:
Artisan, 2004)

*Bread: A Baker's Book of Techniques and Recipes*
by Jeffrey Hamelman (Hoboken, NJ: John Wiley &
Sons, 2004)

*Bread Alone* by Daniel Leader and Judith Blahnik (New
York: William and Morrow, 1993)

*The Bread Baker's Apprentice* by Peter Reinhart
(Berkeley: Ten Speed Press, 2001)

*The Bread Builders* by Alan Scott and Daniel Wing
(White River Junction, VT: Chelsea Green
Publishing, 1999)

*Build Your Own Earth Oven* by Kiko Denzer (Blodgett,
OR: Hand Print Press, 2000)

*From a Baker's Kitchen* by Gail Sher (New York:
Marlowe & Company, 1984–2004)

*How Baking Works* by Paula Figoni (Hoboken, NJ:
John Wiley & Sons, 2007)

*Local Breads* by Daniel Leader and Lauren Chattman
(New York: W. W. Norton, 2007)

*The Taste of Bread* by Raymond Calvel, translated
by Ron Wirtz (Gaithersburg, MD: Aspen Publishers,
2001)

*Whole Grain Breads* by Peter Reinhart (Berkeley:
Ten Speed Press, 2007)

# Glossary

**baker's percentage:** professional standard of calculating weight in a formula; the total flour weight is always considered 100 percent in comparison to the rest of the ingredients

**biga:** Italian-style pre-ferment with a hydration rate of 50 to 60 percent

**bran:** outer portion of the wheat kernel (or berry)

**bulk fermentation:** primary stage of fermentation

**couche:** tightly woven baker's linen used in the proofing of bread

**crumb:** interior portion of the bread

**elasticity:** ability of a dough to spring back from pressure or manipulation; aided by the protein glutenin

**endosperm:** innermost portion of the wheat kernel from which most of the bread flour comes

**enriched:** refers to dough that has a high percentage of fat and sugar

**extensibility:** a dough's ability to be stretched or extended; aided by the protein gliadin

**fermentation:** process of yeast converting sugars into carbon dioxide; gives dough flavour and volume

**folding:** process of hand manipulating dough to build strength during the bulk fermentation, as well as to expel old carbon dioxide and balance out temperature

**germ:** nucleus of the wheat berry where the next generation of the seed is stored

**gliadin:** protein in flour that gives extensibility; aids in forming gluten

**glutenin:** protein in flour that gives elasticity; aids in forming gluten

**gluten:** combinations of proteins that form a web-like matrix and capture gases, giving dough lift and structure

**hydration:** amount of liquids in a dough in relationship to the flour

**lame:** baker's blade used to make incisions in the dough before baking

**lamination:** alternating layers of dough and butter that separate during the baking process

**lean dough:** doughs that contain no additional sugars or fats other than what is naturally present in flour

**malt:** substance derived from barley containing enzymes that are beneficial to the bread-baking process; referred to in bread baking as diastatic malt; can be either liquid or dry, used in the same weight ratio

**old dough:** pre-ferment that is kept from the original dough for an overnight cold fermentation and is added to the next day's dough

**osmotolerant:** form of instant yeast designed to perform better in enriched doughs—doughs that contain sugar and fat, such as brioche or croissant

**oven spring:** last moment of expansion in a loaf of bread that happens in an oven

**peel:** flat tool, usually wooden, that allows the baker to add the bread to or remove it from the oven

**plastic:** softened stage of butter that does not interfere with gluten development

**poolish:** 100 percent hydrated pre-ferment; ideal for baguettes

**pre-ferment:** percentage of dough that is allowed to ferment before mixing the final dough

**preshaping:** initial shaping that takes place to "train" the dough for its final shape

**proofing:** time the loaves are resting right after dividing or before baking

**room temperature:** 70°F to 75°F (21°C to 24°C)

**score:** process of cutting the loaf before it goes into the oven

**shaping:** final forming of a loaf into the desired shape

**simple syrup:** sweet syrup made from water and sugar. Combine one part sugar with one part water in saucepan. Bring to a boil; immediately remove from heat and allow to cool.

**sponge:** pre-ferment that is hydrated at 60 to 63 percent; usually used for sweet dough applications

**transfer peel:** long, thin board used to transfer the baguette from the couche to the peel

**yeast:** single-cell fungus used to ferment bread; takes sugars and transforms them into carbon dioxide and alcohol

# Index

storage, bread, 55
stretch and fold, 32–33, 53
sugar glaze, 153

**T**

tare function, 26
temperature conversions, 165
temperature probe, 33, 38
thermometer/timer, 38
timelines, 166–167
toppings
    cinnamon spice, 156
    crumb, 156
    nut crumb, 156
troubleshooting, 160–164
twist sticks, 75

**W**

water, function of, 20
water bath, baking in, 151
weight conversions, 25, 165
wheat berries, 16
whole wheat dough, 79–85
    pita bread, 84–85
    round rolls, 82
    savoury pizzalets, 83
whole wheat loaf, 84–85
whole wheat flour, baking with, 109

**Y**

yeast, 18–19
yeast conversions, 165

# Acknowledgments

WRITING THIS BOOK has been an incredible journey. It is the result of the help of many people. Without them, I could not have completed this book.

First and foremost, to my wife and partner in this project, Kylee, for spending countless hours taking my knowledge and ideas and putting them into words. I couldn't have done it without her.

To my parents, Maja Rieben and Berni Hitz, whose love, advice, and help allowed me to grow into the person I am today, and to my stepfather, Johnny Rieben, for his enthusiastic appreciation of great food. I also want to thank my mother-in-law, Sherrill Hunnibell, and my sister-in-law, Nadine Rieben, for their love, help, and generosity.

To the entire Baking and Pastry Department Faculty, Culinary Administration, and Staff at Johnson & Wales University, for supporting me through the years with my many crazy projects and putting up with me on a daily basis. I would also like to thank all the students I have had the honor to work with over the years, for inspiring me and making me a better teacher.

A special thank you to Laura Cronin, John Maieli, and Christopher Smith, for spending their precious free time scaling, cleaning, critiquing, sweeping, mopping, carrying, boxing… without them, this book would still be in the making.

To my friend and colleague, Mitch Stamm, for having the answer to my every question and then some.

To my photographer, Ron Manville, for seeing bread in fresh and unexpected ways.

To the people at Quarry Books and particularly my editor, Rochelle Bourgault, for her support, patience, vision, and eloquence.

And finally, to all the bakers that I have had the pleasure of learning from and working with over the years; it is their craft that has brought a sense of fulfillment to my life.

Of course there are many, many more people whose lives have touched me through the years, both personally and professionally—too many to mention here on this page. You know who you are, and I am deeply grateful to you.

## About the Author

CIRIL HITZ is the Department Chair for the International Baking and Pastry Institute at Johnson & Wales University in Providence, Rhode Island. He graduated from the Rhode Island School of Design, after which he returned to his native Switzerland and completed a three-year apprenticeship as a Pastry Chef/Chocolatier. He was first introduced to bread baking while in Europe, which laid the foundation for the skills that led him to where he is today.

Hitz has been recognized nationally and internationally with numerous awards and accomplishments. He was selected as a Top Ten Pastry Chef in America in both 2007 and 2008 by *Pastry Art & Design* magazine. In 2004 he competed in the National Bread and Pastry Team Championship, winning the overall team Gold Medal as well as all individual bread awards. He was a member of the Bread Bakers Guild Team USA that competed at the 2002 Coupe du Monde de la Boulangerie in Paris, where the team captured the silver medal. He has been a guest instructor and expert at many national and international culinary events and schools and serves on the Advisory Board of the Bread Bakers Guild of America.

Ciril Hitz is frequently seen on *The Food Network* and has been featured on the NBC's *The Today Show.* His work has graced the pages of numerous magazines and the interiors of exhibition halls and museums, including COPIA in Napa, California. He is the producer of his own line of educational DVDs. For more information on his work, visit www.breadhitz.com.

## About the Photographer

RON MANVILLE is an award-winning culinary, travel, and lifestyle photographer. Books he has photographed include IACP and James Beard Award winners. He shoots throughout the United States, Canada, and Europe and lives in Nashville, Tennessee, with his wife, Christine. More of his work can be viewed on his website, www.ronmanville.com.